A COLLECTION OF WORDS AND PICTURES
COMMEMORATING GOLF'S CROWN JEWEL

The Ryder Cup Meets The Monster

Foreward by
DOW FINSTERWALD JR.

Written by
BRYON PERRY

The Ryder Cup Meets The Monster

Published by Premiere Publishing LLC
Bingham Farms, Michigan 48025

Copyright 2004 Premiere Publishing LLC
Printed in USA
International Standard Book Number 0-9753526-0-1

Written by:
Bryon A. Perry

Researched and edited by:
Christopher J. Perry

Creative Direction:
Bearclaw Communications LLC

Art Direction:
Gene Renaker

Golf Course Illustrations:
Marc Medrich-theCLIKgroup

The Ryder Cup Meets The Monster was printed on
80# Mead Lustro and supplied by
XPEDEX Seaman Patrick Group
and MeadWestvaco Corporation

Library of Congress Cataloging-in-Publication Data
ISBN 0-9753526-0-1

Printed by Graphic Enterprises Incorporated,
Madison Heights, Michigan

Library of Congress Cataloging-in-Publication Data

Perry, Bryon A.
     The Ryder Cup Meets The Monster / Bryon Perry
          p. cm.
     Includes references and links
     ISBN 0-975-3526-0-1
     1. Historical sports books — Nonfiction. 1. Title
        HSP0000A0A00   2004
   000.0–aa00   04-00000
                              CIP

The Ryder Cup Meets The Monster is an
independently published commemorative for the
35th Ryder Cup Matches. Its content is
neither authorized nor licensed by either the
PGA of America or Oakland Hills Country Club.

Acknowledgements

The author wishes to extend his sincere thanks and appreciation to the following for their assistance in providing words and images used in this publication: sons, Christopher and Mark Perry, The "Zuz", Pamela Jane, the Fred Corcoran Estate, The Portland Golf Club, The Detroit Golf Club, Plum Hollow Golf Club, Royal Birkdale Golf Club, Walton Heath Golf Club, Wentworth Golf Club, Muirfield Village Golf Club, The Massachusetts Golf Association, Phillip Sheldon Golf Pics, The Greenbrier, Christopher John Photography, Southport, The Detroit News, The Detroit Free Press, The World Golf Hall of Fame, Scioto Golf Club, The Champions Club, Worcester Country Club, Royal Lytham and Saint Annes, Pinehurst Country Club, Getty Images, AP Wide World, USGA Archive, Ganton Golf Club, Rick Bochenek – Hogan's Restaurant

Photography Credits

USGA Archive P.P. 34-35-36

AP Wide World Photos P.P. 45-49-72-85-90-92-93-Back Cover

Getty Images P.P. 10-12-18-23-37-38-40-44-48-59-60-65-74-78-79-80-81-82-84-86-87-88-89-94-96-97-Back Cover

Phillip Sheldon P.P. 42-70-71

Selected Bibliography

The Ryder Cup, Golf's Greatest Event
Bob Bubka and Tom Clavin 1999

The Ryder Cup, The Definitive History of Playing For Pride and Country
Colin Jarmin 1999

The Ryder Cup, Seven Decades of Golfing Glory, Drama and Controversy
Dale Concannon 2001

World Golf Hall of Fame

The Detroit Free Press

The Detroit News

Foreward

It's that time again and what a treat we're in for this September. The Ryder Cup matches will be played on the great Oakland Hills South Course. Golf fans will have the opportunity to watch the game's best players competing on one of the world's greatest tournament venues.

The fellows chosen for this year's play will have their hands full competing in this international rivalry. That golf course they call the Monster will be challenging 24 of the world's top competitors on every shot and the match play format will, as always, bring out their best.

The aura of this event has changed since my Dad competed as a player and later as Captain of United States' Ryder Cup team in 1977. But even today, circumstances remain the same. The pressure to win and not let your teammates down will be overwhelming. To me that's what makes the Ryder Cup Matches so special.

Today's biennial matches have gone far beyond being a celebrated media event. They are three days of pressure-packed golf. What's at stake is individual pride and national honor. Again, the key word here is pressure; the likes of which cannot be matched on the weekly tour stops and even the Majors.

Throughout the year, professional golf is about individual performance. Not so in Ryder Cup play. One missed shot could result in your team, and the country you represent, perhaps losing the Cup. Just ask any player whose shot meant winning or losing the Cup. Their experiences remain with them for the rest of their lives.

Naturally I'm cheering for our home team. Regardless who captures the Cup, these matches at Oakland Hills will be the best ever, as the adage goes, 'May the best team win'. For all of us who love this wonderful game and the Ryder Cup, we're in for three days of the best that golf has to offer.

Dow Finsterwald Jr.

Head Golf Professional
Colonial Country Club
Fort Worth, Texas

The Ryder Cup Meets The Monster

There are few events and venues that capture the essence of competition and sport at the highest level. Only in the rarest instances does an opportunity for immortality present itself on hallowed grounds, and in the process, write yet another chapter in golf's long and storied history. The 35th Ryder Cup matches characterize this exceptional moment in time. These matches represent an intersection of the best golfers, competing in the most exciting tournament, at one of the most infamous championship venues in the world.

The Ryder Cup is at its peak of popularity, thanks in part to swelling TV ratings and media attention, controversy and competitive fire rarely seen in professional golf. The personal triumphs and tribulations associated with the Ryder Cup have made it one of the sporting world's most anticipated events, only to be rivaled by the Olympics and the World Cup.

In 2004, the eyes of the world will be fixated on the personal drama and team competition to take place on the Oakland Hills Country Club South Course. This Donald Ross creation hosted its first US Open during the same time period the Ryder Cup was introduced to the golfing world. Over time Oakland Hills has made its mark on golf history having hosted some of the greatest champions, and championship moments, the game has ever seen.

A Mainline Club For Major Competition

Since its opening, the Oakland Hills Country Club has remained one of golf's most consistent venues for major PGA and USGA tournament competition. The Club is one of the few to have two courses designed by famed architect Donald Ross, the mastermind behind other celebrated layouts including Pinehurst #2, Seminole and Oak Hill, among many others. All told, over 100 US National Championships have been played on his designs.

Arguably one of Ross' most famous works is the Oakland Hills South Course, an eighteen-hole masterpiece that was unveiled prior to 1920. It continues to draw accolades as one of the finest and most difficult courses in the world. Carved out of hundreds of oak and maple trees, sitting amid rolling terrain, the South Course is defined by its classic layout, prodigious fairways and deep, well-placed bunkers. All who know the course would agree its most distinguishing characteristic is its fast and severely contoured greens.

Throughout Oakland Hills' rich eighty-eight year existence, virtually anyone affiliated with the PGA, USGA and professional tournament golf at one time or another has competed at Oakland Hills. Shortly after it opened its doors to an enthusiastic membership, the Club hosted its first major

The newspaper article announcing the opening of Oakland Hills Country Club in the Pontiac Press on October 16, 1916.

championship, the 1924 US Open. Oakland Hills would later be recognized as one of America's mainline clubs for professional competition having hosted at least one major tournament event in all but one decade since its opening. In total, Oakland Hills has hosted twelve Majors.

The Farms That Became Famous

At the onset of the Twentieth Century, automobile manufacturing was set to revolutionize the American landscape, and in the process, change the face of Southeast Michigan forever. In 1916, Joseph Mack and Norval Hawkins were making their fortunes in this rapidly expanding industry, much due to Henry Ford and his "Tin Lizzie." Mack, Ford's lead advertising executive, and Hawkins, his first accountant and sales manager, joined an array of wealthy businessmen who were responsible for creating country clubs in and around Detroit, Michigan.

Mack and Hawkins, along with a few investors, purchased some 450-plus acres of rolling pasture and orchards that comprised the Miller, Spicer and Leach farms along Maple Road in Birmingham. The farms would be the site of a first-class golf course and country club for friends and business associates to congregate. On October 17, 1916, these two men and 46 others met at the Detroit Athletic Club to hold the first Board of Directors meeting of the Oakland Hills Country Club. The club's first members, totaling 140, each paid $250 to join.

Automobile Capital Becomes Club Capital

As Detroit became the automobile capital of the world, entrepreneurs and inventors alike created the industry's most recognized corporate names such as General Motors, Ford and Chrysler. Original inventors such as Dodge, Ford, Fisher, Chevrolet and others saw their identities evolve into some of industry's most recognizable brand names.

A famous farm spawns a famous finish: Oakland Hills' 18th Hole.

Ben Hogan (pictured above) during one of many championship moments at Oakland Hills.

In one fashion or another, automotive pioneers were instrumental in establishing country clubs in the area that became playgrounds and social settings for Detroit's rich and famous. Establishments such as The Detroit Golf Club, the Country Club of Detroit, Pine Lake Country Club, Henry Ford's Dearborn Country Club, Plum Hollow Country Club, Western Golf and Country Club, Franklin Country Club and Bloomfield Hills Country Club were all founded during the same era. Interestingly, Donald Ross was the designer of a great many of them, and in all, his layouts can be seen in over 200 courses throughout the state of Michigan.

Pine Lake Country Club, not far from Oakland Hills, was originally named, The Automobile Club of Detroit and later became an affiliate of the Automobile Club of America. Some of its original founders' included Dodge and Ford. In 1921, the Club was renamed Pine Lake Country Club.

Donald Ross

"The Lord Intended This For A Golf Course..."

Following the initial board meeting, work commenced immediately to build the golf course. At the December board meeting in 1916, Joseph Mack detailed construction plans for the links and announced that he engaged the services of Donald James Ross, the preeminent golf course architect from Royal Dornoch, Scotland. Upon seeing the farmland that would become Oakland Hills, Ross proclaimed, "The Lord intended this for a golf course!"

Built prior to 1920, Ross' original footprint and routing of the South Course remains virtually the same today. While many alterations have been made to the original design, there has never been a suggestion that could improve its basic plan. Ross, the most prolific designer of his day, went on to design more than 400 other golf courses throughout the United States. When complete, Oakland Hills would be remembered as one of his greatest triumphs and most enduring efforts.

Beyond the genius defined by his Oakland Hills design, many marveled at his ability to develop so many course designs at one time – a major challenge given that course construction was done by hand and with horse drawn plows.

Enter the little known name of Ernie Wey. An employee of nearby Bloomfield Hills Country Club, Wey would offer his services to Ross and oversee the daily construction of Ross' designs in and around Detroit. Wey worked tirelessly at maintaining the integrity of Ross' land usage, and often his impossible deadlines. Little history has been recorded about Ernie Wey but he is due much credit for the execution and completion of Ross' work.

Donald Ross, a former club maker and golf professional from Dornoch, Scotland, is still considered the preeminent name in golf course architecture. After immigrating to the United States he eventually set up his permanent headquarters in a modest pro shop at Pinehurst, North Carolina where he designed the Pinehurst No. 2 course, another of his greatest achievements. Comfortable in his North Carolina surroundings, he welcomed many as both a club maker and golf course designer. Ross lived out his years at Pinehurst and died in 1948.

Be Sure To "Stop And Smell The Flowers Along The Way"

ollowing the selection of Donald Ross, Mack and Hawkins next sought out the Club's first golf professional. Ross attempted to play a part in this as well, recommending a little known player by the name of Mike Brady. Joe Mack had his own ideas. In May of 1918, Mack entered into negotiations with Walter Hagen, the man who would become Oakland Hills' first head professional and the most popular and golfer of his time. Even more than his tournament record, which would boast five PGA's, two US Opens, and four British Open Championships between 1914 and 1927, Hagen would be remembered for his flamboyant style and his famous creed, "Never hurry, never worry and be sure to smell the flowers along the way."

For Joe Mack, it wasn't an easy sell. Mack's representative visited Hagen at his residence in Rochester, New York knowing full well not to return without Hagen's signature on the carefully written and generous contract. Eventually Hagen accepted Mack's offer consisting of a $300 monthly salary, along with profits from the sale of golf equipment and merchandise. Hagen took the position as head golf professional vowing to provide his "entire time and personal services to the club." By 1927, Mack and Hawkins unveiled a country club and golf course that would rival any other in the nation. Their Club was set to occupy an honored place in golf history for decades to come.

Oakland Hills first golf professional, the legendary Walter Hagen

Excellence And Wartime Exhibitions

18   L+   SPORTS   THE NEW YORK TIMES, MONDAY, AUGUST 9, 1943.   SPORTS

Ryder Cup Golfers Rout Hagen Team By Taking Six of Eight Singles Matches

The New York Times article reporting on the famous Red Cross Exhibitions.

All country clubs possess their own unique culture and by no means is Oakland Hills an exception. The Club from the onset created a culture based exclusively on golf and championship competition. The selections of Donald Ross and Walter Hagen set a precedent for excellence that would exemplify Oakland Hills for the next eighty-plus years. A look into the Club's history confirms its members know how to host championships of the highest caliber and raise significant proceeds in the process. Since its inception in 1916, Oakland Hills staged a major golf tournament in every decade but one, that being the 1940's during World War II. During this period in time Oakland Hills hosted the first in a series of exhibitions by the US Ryder Cup team led by its original Playing Captain, Walter Hagen.

A Parallel Vision

At the same time Mack and Hawkins were creating Oakland Hills, thousands of miles away an easy going businessman named Samuel Ryder was selling flower seeds to the British masses for a penny a package. For Samuel Ryder, his business proceeds provided the means to devote time to his passion for golf. It was Ryder's vision that led to a goodwill competition that would eventually become the Ryder Cup.

In 1926, Ryder decided to arrange a friendly competition between British and American golf professionals. Testimony to Ryder's passion for the game, these matches were one of few competitions founded on camaraderie and goodwill, rather than money.

Although Mack, Hawkins and Ryder possessed differing agendas, these three men were visionaries who shared a common enthusiasm for the game. The Ryder Cup Matches would be established at approximately the same time Oakland Hills would host its first of six US Opens.

Mack, Hawkins and Ryder were separated by thousands of miles and probably never met, but decades later their efforts would culminate with Ryder Cup play at Mack and Hawkins' Club north of Detroit, Michigan.

The Detroit Golf Club's stately clubhouse. (above)
Walter Hagen

Hagen came out of retirement and pitted his team of Byron Nelson, Jimmy Picard and Sam Snead against Gene Sarazen, Jimmy Demaret and a young Ben Hogan. The proceeds from these unofficial matches, and subsequent exhibitions staged by the US Ryder Cup team, would be directed to the Red Cross War effort.

Following the first Red Cross exhibitions at Oakland Hills, the Ryder Cup team held additional matches to raise proceeds for the War. In 1941 and 1942 the matches were played at the Detroit Golf Club, another Donald Ross, thirty-six hole layout. The legendary Bobby Jones fielded a team of amateurs that bested Walter Hagen's US Ryder Cup team. The following year in 1943, the matches descended upon Plum Hollow Country Club in Southfield, Michigan. Plum Hollow's own Jimmy Demaret was one of the qualifiers. Among the many celebrities was Bing Crosby in a gallery of over 16,000 spectators. These two-day matches raised over $35,000 for the American Red Cross. The three Detroit area country clubs all shared a part in Ryder Cup history along with playing a role in maintaining its biennial tradition.

The Monster Comes Of Age

The Oakland Hills clubhouse overlooks the Monster.

During the Club's storied eighty-plus year history, it has enjoyed countless milestone events. Perhaps the most significant began prior to the 1951 US Open. Equipment improvements necessitated major changes to championship courses that would continue hosting major tournaments. The same held true of Oakland Hills which had been selected as the host site for its third US Open in 1951.

In preparation for the '51 Open, the Club made a decision to engage the highly regarded golf course designer, Robert Trent Jones. Jones was charged to enhance Ross' classic layout and address the current demands of tournament competition. His task was to challenge the game's best players and their newer and technologically advanced equipment while not compromising Ross' layout and design.

To the dismay of many contestants, the '51 Open would be played on a radically different golf course than most could have ever expected. With the approval of the Oakland Hills' Executive Committee and the United States Golf Association, Jones' re-work was considered the most daunting challenge ever presented for a USGA competition.

In the months prior to the tournament, the Club unveiled what many players regarded as their worst nightmare. The South Course now had narrow landing areas – in some cases a mere 25 yards wide – that were surrounded by deep punishing rough. There were also 120 new bunkers strategically positioned to guard landing areas and greens, many of them severe, deep traps with overhanging lips. The last five holes were particularly brutal and became known as the "Fearsome Fivesome."

Jones was on a mission. His belief in enhancing the course was, "Every hole should be a hard par and an easy bogey." He, and the contestants, got more than they bargained for. Jones set out and created hell on earth for the US Open contestants. After completion of the first round, outcries from the contestants were echoed in headlines throughout the country. After three rounds Ben Hogan, the eventual winner, was struggling and stood at ten strokes over par. It took a remarkable final round 67 by Hogan to win the championship. His total score of 287 was seven shots over par. The course that Trent Jones created prevailed over every player competing that week. Par had defeated the entire field of contestants – 162-0.

The history books tell that this tournament re-defined what it took to be the Open Champion. It became a survival of the fittest and was considered a watershed year for US Open play. Ben Hogan, one of the fiercest competitors in the history of the game, literally fought his way to the Championship on the most demanding golf course of its time.

Following his victory Hogan was reputedly quoted as saying, "I brought this course, this monster to its knees." Others attributed the reference to the New York World Telegram's syndicated sports cartoonist Willard Mullin whose his pen and ink drawing depicted a dragon looming over Ben Hogan decreeing Oakland Hills as a monster. Whichever version is preferred, the name stuck. From that day forward the Oakland Hills South Course was referred to as, "The Monster."

Hogan's mastery at one of the Monster's cavernous bunkers.

Another Ross Gem Is Literally Steps Away

Oakland Hills' courses are among Ross' finest achievements.

Given the notoriety of the South Course it was a little known fact until the mid-sixties that Donald Ross had designed another gem literally steps away from his more famous venue.

Ross had also been the original designer of Oakland Hills' "other" layout, the Oakland Hills North Course, originally named North Hills. Ross felt, with careful attention, this course could compare with some of the best in the world. Its landscape is as diverse as the layout of the holes.

It was the early intent of Oakland Hills' members to operate the North Course as a daily fee course. In the mid-1960s they chose to take it private to accommodate the Club's growing membership. Oakland Hills now shared the distinction with another club in the area, the Detroit Golf Club, of having two layouts designed by Donald Ross.

In the early '60s Robert Trent Jones' vision for toughening Oakland Hills was called upon once again. This time the task would be reworking and upgrading the North Course. Within five years, what was considered Oakland Hills' other course became one of this area's most challenging and enjoyable layouts. Still today, the old North Hills continues to be the subject of considerable debate by Oakland Hills members – many of whom believe the North Course from the blue tees can be every bit as challenging as the South.

Hogan Commemorates 75 Years At Oakland Hills

In 1991, 75 years after the establishment of Oakland Hills, the Club celebrated its Diamond Jubilee by hosting its second USGA Men's Senior Open. In planning for the '91 event, the Club chose Ben Hogan as its Honorary Chairman to commemorate the 40th anniversary of his 1951 Open victory. Although ill health prevented Hogan from attending, a commendation letter said it all. Ben shared his reflections of that tournament with members of Oakland Hills during their visit to Hogan's home in Fort Worth, Texas. To Hogan the final round of the '51 Open was, in his opinion, one of his finest ever.

BEN HOGAN   P O Box 11276   **Ft. Worth, Texas 76110**

Dear Friends:

As I begin to write this letter, my mind immediately wanders back 40 years to the 1951 U.S.Open Tournament played at Oakland Hills. I was fortunate to win the tournament with some of the best rounds of golf that I have ever played. It was a tough course, but it was such a pleasure to "bring that monster to its knees." Oh, how I would love to experience, just once more, my days of golf at Oakland Hills during the 1951 U.S.Open. Those days are gone now, but I still cherish the memories of my times at Oakland Hills.

I would like to thank the U.S.Senior Open Championship officials at Oakland Hills for bestowing on me the honor of being named the Honorary Chairman of this year's 1991 Senior Open. I know it will be a very successful tournament, and I wish all of the participants good luck.

Good luck and congratulations are also extended to Oakland Hills Country Club on its 75th anniversary. Your club has earned its place in golf history and I know all of your members are proud to be a part of this wonderful establishment.

I appreciate your honoring me as you have, and with my very best wishes to all of you, I am

Sincerely

Ben Hogan

Ben Hogan's letter presented to Oakland Hills members.

The Plan To Secure The Cup

As a consistent stop for major tournament competition, the Club's directors and officers regularly reviewed opportunities to showcase their club and its South Course through another major event. But before the turn of the millennium relatively few were aware of a bolder, more exciting opportunity under consideration. Planning was underway to capture a new event, one that was emerging as the biggest and most high profile spectacle in all of golf. Oakland Hills' reputation as one of the nation's mainline clubs for site selection had usually been a favorable asset when future tournament venues were chosen. But the Club's officers knew history and heritage would not be enough to secure the crown jewel of international golf.

As the Club's planners were considering their next venture, Oakland Hills had already embarked on the most ambitious clubhouse and site renovation in its history.

In 1917, C. Howard Crane submitted the plan for Oakland Hills' original clubhouse modeled after George Washington's Mt. Vernon. Four years later the clubhouse was opened to the membership at an eye-opening cost of $650,000. In years to come the clubhouse would grow in size and become an imposing building that still stands prominently over the South Course today.

Rather than tear down and start anew, the membership went forward with renovations without diminishing its original, historic character. In the process considerable thought was given to better position the Club for accommodating future professional championships. Not only did the stately clubhouse undergo a complete restoration from the ground up, a new and larger pro shop, separate cart storage facility and an impressive first tee staging area were also created. The Club closed its doors for over a year, and over $15 million dollars later, a new Oakland Hills was unveiled to its proud membership.

The renovations went beyond the clubhouse and on to the course as well. After the conclusion of the 2002 Men's National Amateur, the Club began addressing alterations to the golf course. The most significant change included construction plans for a new forward tee on the 6th hole, normally a par four played at 360 yards in past tournaments. With the new tee under consideration, contestants will approach No. 6 as a 305-yard, reachable par four that can require a more strategic and exciting decision off the tee.

Other renovations under consideration included newly repaired roads and staging on the North Course to withstand machinery and trucks needed for the construction of bleachers, hospitality tents, merchandising venues and concessions required for major tournament operations.

Prior to the millenium, Oakland Hills approached the PGA of America to host their crown jewel, the 35th Ryder Cup Matches. Having already conducted two successful PGA Championships in 1972 and 1979, Oakland Hills was no stranger to the people at the PGA. The experience of working ten prior events and a vast pool of experienced and enthusiastic volunteers were two of many compelling reasons for the PGA of America to take a serious look at what the members from Birmingham, Michigan had to offer.

In the fall of 1998, the PGA of America made their choice for the 2003 Matches. They elected once again to have golf history be played out at Oakland Hills. The events of 9/11 forced the postponement to 2004. Eventually, it would be a fitting site for the best to meet the best.

Oakland Hills' South Course stands ready for the PGA's Crown Jewel.

Major Championships
At Oakland Hills

1924
US Open

1929
US Women's National Amateur

1937
US Open

1951
US Open

1961
US Open

1972
PGA Championship

1979
PGA Championship

1981
US Senior Open

1985
US Open

1991
US Senior Open

1996
US Open

2002
US Men's National Amateur

1924 US Open
June 5th & 6th, 1924

Cyril Walker

Par 72					
Cyril Walker	74	74	74	75	297
Robert T. Jones*	74	73	75	78	300
William E. Melhorn	72	75	76	78	301
Robert A. Cruickshank	72	72	76	73	303
Walter Hagen	75	75	76	77	303

* Amateur

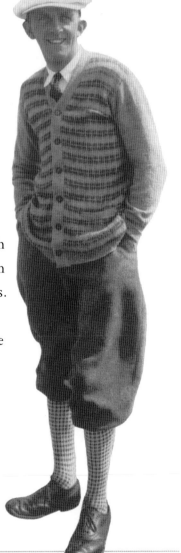

Little more than five years old, Oakland Hills held the 1924 US Open. The favorite was Bobby Jones who was the tournament's defending champion. He had an impressive list of contenders, Tommy Armour, Leo Diegel, Bill Melhorn, and the Club's first professional, Walter Hagen. Ironically, the winner, a rank outsider, predicted his own victory. Cyril Walker, a 118-pound Englishman, proclaimed in an interview that a relatively unknown player would win the tournament. Walker fulfilled his prediction by besting runner up Jones by three shots. Jones' nemesis, which probably cost him the tournament, was the tenth hole. He never took less than bogey in all four rounds. Walter Hagen finished 15 over par and had to settle for a fourth place tie with Bobby Cruickshank.

1929 US Women's National Amateur
September 30th - October 5th, 1924

Glenna Collete Vare

The year 1929 would mark the only time Oakland Hills hosted a Women's Amateur. The winner, Glenna Collete Vare, was considered the female equivalent of Bobby Jones. Like Jones, Vare was considered one of the greatest amateur players of all time. Oakland Hills boasted one of its own, Violet Hanley, who reached the quarterfinals. Vare's amateur career eventually spanned four decades. She played in her first Amateur in 1919 and last in 1947.

1937 US Open
June 10th & 12th, 1937

Par 72					
Ralph Guldahl	71	69	72	69	281
Sam Snead	69	73	70	71	283
Robert A. Cruichshank	73	73	67	72	285
Henry E. Cooper	72	70	73	71	286
Ed Dudley	70	70	67	72	279

Ralph Guldahl

The 41st US Open Championship was won by Ralph Guldahl, who just one year earlier threatened to give up the game. This tournament was played on the longest course on record at a grueling 7,037 yards. Sam Snead at age 24 was one of the favorites heading into the tournament. Nearly every player to win a major championship in the Thirties was on hand, but destiny was pointing to the two young players, Snead and Guldhal. Throughout the fourth round it was a two-man duel. Snead couldn't respond to Guldahl's 69 and finished runner up, two behind Guldahl's seven under 281. This was the first of many times Sam Snead would be denied the US Open, the only major championship that eluded him throughout his entire career. Ralph Guldahl would successfully defend his title by winning again in 1938.

1951 US Open
June 14ʰ & 15ʰ, 1951

Ben Hogan

Par 70		
Ben Hogan	76 73 71 67	287
Clayton Heafner	72 75 73 69	289
A. D. (Bobby) Locke	73 71 74 73	291
Lloyd Mangrum	75 75 74 70	294
Julius Boros	74 74 71 74	293

In 1951, Oakland Hills unveiled its reworked and controversial golf course. By now Sam Snead had become known for his Open jinx but remained one of the favorites along with South African, Bobby Locke and Lloyd Mangrum. When all was said and done, Ben Hogan was the sole player to beat par and won one of the most memorable tournaments of his life. Said Hogan, "I'm not a machine, only a golfer, and Oakland Hills was designed for some kind of super golfer that I've never seen yet. I honestly feel this is the hardest golf course in the world, I haven't played them all, but this is the toughest I've ever seen."

1961 US Open
June 15th & 17th, 1961

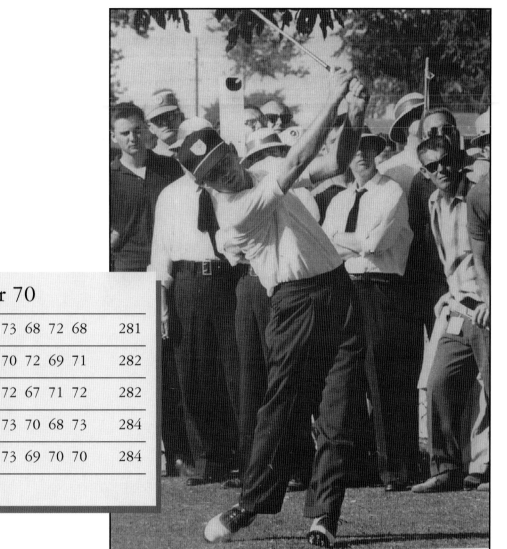

Gene Littler

Par 70			
Gene Littler	73 68 72 68	281
Bob Goalby	70 72 69 71	282
Doug Sanders	72 67 71 72	282
Mike Souchak	73 70 68 73	284
Jack Nicklaus*	73 69 70 70	284
* Amateur		

Into the 1961 US Open, Arnold Palmer sat as defending champion following his thrilling win at Cherry Hills. Palmer was runner up at the '61 Masters and the odds on favorite to win. A young amateur, Jack Nicklaus, runner up to Palmer at Cherry Hills was also one to watch. One nobody counted on as a contender was Gene Littler. His winnings were a mere $116 coming into the tournament and had been frustrated for six consecutive years. He edged Bob Goalby by one shot to take the 61st US Open title. Yes, the Monster was played with less difficulty than in '51 but Gene Littler was the closest player to break par.

1972 PGA Championship

July 31st & August 5th, 1972

Par 70					
Gary Player	71	71	67	72	281
Tommy Aaron	71	71	70	71	283
Jim Jamieson	69	72	72	70	283
Billy Casper	73	70	67	74	284
Raymond Floyd	69	71	74	70	284

Gary Player

A different championship debuted at Oakland Hills in 1972. This time it was the 54th PGA Championship. Jack Nicklaus stood as defending champion and Arnold Palmer continued to suffer his PGA Championship jinx. Palmer had finished runner up in '64, '68 and '70. Again, it was not to be. The championship was won by South African star, Gary Player. Player's approach shot on the Monster's signature hole, the 16th, provided one of the most dramatic moments in major tournament history; a blind second shot to within four feet of the pin. Said Player, "It was one of the best shots of my career."

1979 PGA
July 30ᵗʰ - August 5ᵗʰ, 1979

Par 70						
David Graham	69	68	70	65	272
Ben Crenshaw	69	67	69	67	272
Rex Caldwell	67	70	66	71	274
Ron Strek	68	71	69	68	276
Gibby Gilbert	69	72	68	69	278

David Graham

In 1979, the PGA Championship returned with a group of young lions some of which were to challenge the Monster for the first time. At the tournament's conclusion, there were 140-sub par or even par rounds. Add to that, fifteen players beat Gary Player's 1972 winning total of 281. Final round drama unfolded when Ben Crenshaw and Australia's David Graham wound up tied at 272. Crenshaw and Graham proceed to a three-hole sudden death playoff. Graham displayed one of the best clutch putting performances in major golf history en route to victory. Oakland Hills put on one of its greatest parties. Total attendance was 145,102 beating the prior PGA record by 31,000 attendees.

1981 US Senior Open
July 9ᵗʰ -12ᵗʰ, 1981

Par 70				
Arnold Palmer	72 76 68 73			289
Bob Stone	72 71 74 72			289
Billy Casper	72 75 76 78			301
Art Wall	72 72 76 78			303
Gene Littler	75 75 76 77			303
Play Off	July 13,1981			
Arnold Palmer	70			
Bob Stone	74			
Billy Casper	77			

Arnold Palmer

The establishment of the Senior Tour brought back popular heroes from days gone by. The Senior Tour, a phenomenon of its time, gave greater prominence, popularity and exposure to the US Senior Open. And who better to battle his way to the championship in 1981 than the legend himself, Arnold Palmer. After a slow start, Palmer fought his way back to a three-way tie with Billy Casper, the man who denied him a US Open bid in 1966 at the Olympic Club, and club pro Bob Stone. In a Monday playoff, Casper and Stone fell by the wayside as Palmer mounted one of his patented charges and etched his name into Oakland Hills and USGA history. He became the first player to win the US Amateur, US Open and US Senior Open.

1985 US Open
June 13th - 16th, 1985

Par 70		
Andy North	70 65 70 74	279
Chen Tze Chung	65 69 68 77	280
Denis Watson	72 65 69 70	280
Dave Barr	70 68 70 72	280
Lanny Wadkins	70 72 60 70	282

Andy North

The US Open returned to Oakland Hills for the fifth time in 1985. Unfortunately, many of golf's marquee names failed to make the 36-hole cut. Nonetheless, the tournament never lacked the drama typically associated with a US Open championship. A relatively unknown name will be remembered as much as the eventual winner, Andy North, the only contestant to finish the tournament under par. Two of the 85th Open's most memorable shots came from T. C. Chen of Taiwan. In the first round Chen double eagled the par five second hole, a rare achievement in itself. He would be most remembered for his travails on Sunday when he managed to double hit his greenside chip at No. 5 and make a quadruple bogey eight. Remarkably, Chen gathered his wits finishing one shot behind, Andy North. During the final round, North, Chen, Dave Barr and Denis Watson all took turns at giving the Open away. Fortunately for Andy North, the Monster bit the least. With the 85th Open in the books, Oakland Hills now shared the distinction with three other clubs of having hosted five US Opens.

1991 US Senior Open
July 25th - 28th, 1991

Jack Nicklaus

Par 70					
Jack Nicklaus	72	69	70	71	282
Juan Rodriguez	73	68	70	71	282
Al Geiberger	71	70	72	70	283
Jim Dent	73	72	72	67	284
Lee Trevino	70	72	68	74	284
Play Off					
Nicklaus	65				
Rodriguez	69				

The 1991 US Senior Open marked another memorable competition at Oakland Hills. The tournament featured some of golf's greatest names, but would be remembered for final day heroics and one of the most memorable rounds ever played at the Club. On no. 18 in Sunday's round, Chi Chi Rodriguez hit a sweeping hook from the fairway to within a few feet of the cup. His final-hole birdie would force a Monday playoff with Jack Nicklaus, who had struggled like all others to break par throughout the tournament. Come Monday's round, break par he did, carding a remarkable, course-record 65 to beat Rodriguez for the championship. With his first victory at Oakland Hills Jack Nicklaus would add another chapter to an illustrious history, joining Ben Hogan, Gary Player and Arnold Palmer as tournament champions at the Club.

1996 US Open
June 13th - 16th, 1996

Par 70		
Steve Jones	74 66 69 69	278
Davis Love III	71 69 70 69	279
Tom Lehman	71 72 65 71	279
John Morse	68 74 65 73	280
Ernie Els	72 67 72 70	281
Jim Furyk	72 69 70 70	281

Steve Jones

The US Open competition, by its nature, always seems to present golf fans with drama and excitement, especially due to the extremely difficult conditions set forth by the USGA. 1996 was no exception, the winner would be decided on the 18th hole of the final round with Tom Lehman, Davis Love III and Steve Jones battling for the title. Lehman drilled his tee shot into a fairway bunker leaving him an impossible shot to the green. A two and a half-foot downhill putt stood between Davis and the Championship. He missed, and with a three putt, his hopes were dashed. For Steve Jones, an unlikely contender, par was all that was needed to secure the 85th Open Championship.

2002 US Amateur
August 19th - 25th, 2002

Ricky Barnes

In 2002, Oakland Hills hosted the US Amateur for the first time. In doing so it became one of few clubs in America to host all USGA Major Men's Championships. The field for the 102nd Amateur Championship did its best to challenge what used to be a course noted for its length. Equipment and talent shortened the course, but Oakland Hill's difficult conditions again prevailed. On the last day, the championship came down to Hunter Mahan from McKinney, Texas and a gritty Californian named Ricky Barnes. On Sunday afternoon, the Monster smiled on Barnes who defeated Mahan in a close fought match before a crowd of over 24,000 people. In winning the Amateur at Oakland Hills, Barnes placed himself in the impressive company of Palmer, Hogan, Nicklaus, Player, Littler, Guldahl, Walker, North, Jones, Graham and Vare, all major championship winners at Oakland Hills.

Oakland Hills' signature hole, the famous 16th, has challenged golf's greatest names in the 12 major tournaments.

"We must do this again."

– *Samuel Ryder, 1926*

The History of Golf's Crown Jewel

The Modern Day Ryder Cup

"You've played all over the world. You've played in Majors. But this is the only event I know of that will make your legs shake."

— *Tom Watson*

Every two years the world's top golf professionals go to battle over one the most coveted honors in all sports – The Ryder Cup. Those fortunate to play Ryder Cup Matches are confronted with an entirely opposite set of circumstances from what they are accustomed to on the professional tour. They compete not for prize money or individual acclaim, but as team fighting for honor, pride and country.

To compete in the Ryder Cup, first and foremost, the player's birthplace must be in the United States, Great Britain or Continental Europe. This cross-Atlantic connection is one of the few Ryder Cup rules that

haven't changed since 1927. Modifications were made to extend European team selection beyond Great Britain, and today individuals are chosen based on place of birth as well as performance in tournament competition.

Golfers who participate are subject to an emotional roller coaster that is synonymous with Ryder Cup play. According to Johnny Miller, nothing in golf compares to competing, and coping, with the intensity of these matches. "The four major championships combined don't evoke as much self-doubt and passion as this biennial competition." Regardless of world ranking or stature in the game, no player escapes the heavy pressure and anticipation heading into the event. "You've played all over the world. You've played in Majors," notes Tom Watson. "But this is the only event I know of that will make your legs shake."

Although the Ryder Cup was born from one man's vision based on goodwill and camaraderie, in more recent years it has evolved into a competition so fierce the matches hardly resemble what Samuel Ryder originally proposed in the early 1920's.

The Seeds Of International Competition

The conception for cross-Atlantic competition began as early as 1920. While accounts vary on the origins of the Ryder Cup, American S.P. Jermain, representatives from The Glasgow Herald and James Hartnett of *Golf Illustrated* all proposed that international matches take place between United States and British golf professionals.

Historians confirm that the seeds for the Ryder Cup were firmly planted in 1926 through an informal competition at the Wentworth Golf Club in Surrey, England. That year a group of Americans, led by Walter Hagen, agreed to a match in advance of the British Open at Royal Lytham and St. Annes. The American team was soundly defeated, 13 to 1. While the British team celebrated its decisive victory, Samuel Ryder took note and uttered his famous words, "We must do this again."

Through copious research, Phillip Truett of the Walton Heath Golf Club accounted for the Ryder Cup's actual start date along with Samuel Ryder's influence in a March 2000 article he penned for "Through the Green," the periodical from the Golf Collector's Society.

The Ryder Cup
by Philip Truett

WHEN WAS the true start date of this match? Look in most handbooks and you will read that the the first match was played in the USA in 1927. Some acknowledge that there was an informal match at Wentworth in 1926.

Sam Ryder's own daughter, Joan, told the story of her father giving a champagne party after this match and being persuaded by Duncan, Mitchell and Hagen to give a trophy. Likewise, in Peter Ward's history of Camedown GC, he quotes Eddie Whitcombe who remembered George Duncan 'taking advantage of the euphoria created by the victory (the British Isles had won by a substantial margin), to persuade Samuel Ryder to promise a cup for an official match'.

I believe the true story needs to be told. The Past Captains of Verulam Golf Club (Sam Ryder's home club) are now aware of it, following my talk to them about Sam Ryder's influence on Professional golf and I have their permission to share it with a wider audience!

As early as 1925, when it was announced that there would be a match between the British Isles and the USA at Wentworth the following year, George Greenwood writing in the *Daily Telegraph*, said that the Ryder brothers were 'two keen golfers and enthusiastic sportsmen who originated the idea of an annual match between American and British golfers of front rank'. Note there was no mention of a cup.

Now we must go forward to *The Times* of April and June 1926 and Michael Hobbs' definitive history of the Ryder Cup, published in 1989. He announces that the 1926 match should be considered the first match based upon these *Times* articles he had discovered. This prompts Peter Alliss, in his foreword, to say that he must now correct people when they talk about 1927 being the first year.

The two articles in question were as follows:

Monday, April 26th 1926. "The 'Ryder' Trophy... Mr S. Ryder, of St. Albans, has presented a trophy for annual competition between teams of British and American professionals. The first match for the trophy is to take place at Wentworth on June 4th and 5th...."

Wednesday, June 2nd 1926. "American Professionals arrive....The first important match in which they will take part is against a team of British professionals for the Ryder Cup at Wentworth next Friday and Saturday...."

To support the above, the monthly magazine *Golfing* for June 1926 (no doubt published in late May) announced that "Mr.S.Ryder, of St.Albans, has offered a challenge trophy.....a professional equivalent of the Walker Cup...." *Golf Monthly* ran a similar article.

Hobbs speculates why the trophy wasn't presented and why 1926 has never been considered the first match. He puts two ideas forward. Firstly, the trophy wasn't ready (it has a 1927 hallmark). Secondly, there was a problem over the representation of the US side. Over half the players were ex patriots.

As is so often the case, *Golf Illustrated* had the answer all along. Their edition of June 11th of 1926 made the following announcement:

"The Ryder Cup.... Owing to the uncertainty of the situation following the strike (this was the General Strike) in which it was not known until a few days ago how many American professionals would be visiting Great Britain, Mr J. Ryder (sic) decided to withhold the cup which he has offered for annual competition between the professionals of Great Britain and America. Under these circumstances the Wentworth Club provided the British players with gold medals to mark the inauguration of this great international match".

So there, once and for all, is what really happened. I do not believe Sam Ryder used the strike as a convenient excuse. He would not have been embarrassed without a trophy to present. After all, it didn't put off the Prestwick members in 1872, when the Claret Jug wasn't ready!

As a footnote, and as a lesson for all of us interested in the history of the game, the above story emphasises the importance of GETTING IT RIGHT! Once something is in print, it can always be quoted and, if it isn't correct, the mistake will be perpetuated. After all, it was only in June 1931, just five years after the event, that in the very same *Golf Illustrated* 'a special correspondent' talks about 1927 being the first match because "the Cup wasn't ready".

Philip Truett
January 2000

She said: "I am a-weary;
I cannot make my bed,
Nor help with the preserving,
Nor dust my room," she said.

And, leaping from the hammock,
She seized her bag of sticks,
And did the eighteen holes in just
Exactly ninety-six.

From A REDDITCH DIRECTORY OF 1910 sent in by John Weston

A Legend In The Making

Samuel Ryder, then Mayor of St. Albans

> "I trust the effects of these matches will be to influence a cordial, friendly, and peaceful feeling throughout the whole civilized world. I look upon the Royal and Ancient game as being a powerful force that influences the best things in humanity."
>
> -- Samuel Ryder in a BBC broadcast in 1927

Ryder grew up in Manchester, England and later made a fortune as a seed merchant selling packages by the penny. Before the turn of the century, Ryder moved his family to St. Albans, England where he would become Mayor. As a city servant, Ryder became a fixture in his community and underwrote many charitable organizations. In conjunction with his professional pursuits Ryder became enamored with golf, taking up the game in his early fifties. As a natural leader, Ryder became Captain at his home club where he dedicated much energy to organizing and staging competitive tournaments.

After the completion of the 1926 matches, Ryder was clearly interested in the creation of an ongoing international competition between Britain and the United States. While the British team celebrated its victory, he questioned why the competitors showed so little interest in getting to know each other off the golf course. In Ryder's opinion there was far too little social interaction. He felt friendship was just as important to the game as the competition itself.

The following year Ryder and his colleagues made good on their pledge to "do it again." True to his commitment, Ryder commissioned the Mappin & Webb Company to create a gold cup that would go to the winning team. The trophy, which stood seventeen inches tall and weighed just four pounds, was quite unimposing when compared to the British Open's Claret Jug. The Cup's cost was shared between Ryder himself, *Golf Illustrated* magazine and the Royal and Ancient Golf Club.

Being an astute businessman, Ryder took great interest in the integrity of the matches that would later bear his name. He arranged for a Deed of Trust to be drawn up defining the competition's format and rules that would govern play. Upon the Deed's completion, Ryder's family, along with representatives of the British PGA and the PGA of America, signed the document, which led to "official" Ryder Cup play.

Ryder's Deed of Trust called for two days of matches — the first being foursomes and four ball competition and the second devoted to singles play. A total of twelve points would be awarded. This two day, twelve-point format continued until 1961.

Samuel Ryder's vision and commitment resulted in the first official Ryder Cup Matches in 1927. Led by Ryder and Walter Hagen, the organizers chose the United States as the site for their inaugural event. The plan was to contest the matches at Worcester Country Club near Boston, Massachusetts.

Economics played a pivotal role in establishing the '27 matches. In the United States golf professionals competed for prize money, were paid for their services, and in some instances, backed financially by wealthy businessmen. This certainly wasn't the case in England. The British professionals were far from able to incur expenses associated with overseas travel. Its professionals returned from tournament competitions to full time jobs in their golf shops. They tended to their stores earning meager wages in the process.

Ryder and his associates would need to devise a way to fund the trans-Atlantic trip. Showing full support for the matches, *Golf Illustrated* petitioned Britain's golf clubs for donations. The country's golfing elite showed little interest in these unfamiliar competitions. Consequently the magazine underwrote the majority of the trip.

The British team spent six difficult days at sea. Upon arrival they were in no shape to compete. Nevertheless, the Brits declined the American's offer to delay the competition and declared themselves ready to go.

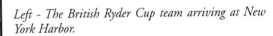

Left - The British Ryder Cup team arriving at New York Harbor.

Below - The victorious United States Ryder Cup team.

1927 Ryder Cup Teams

Great Britain and Ireland - *Ted Ray-Playing Captain, Aubrey Boomer, Archie Compston, George Duncan, Arthur Havers, Herbert Jolly, Fred Robson, Charles Whitcombe, George Gadd*

USA - *Walter Hagen-Playing Captain, Leo Diegle, Johnny Farrell, Johnny Golden, Bill Melhorn, Gene Sarazen, Joe Turnesa, Al Watrous, Al Espinosa*

The inaugral Ryder Cup program

One of Ryder's mandates was that the teams get to know each other better in advance of the competition. Introduced to America's social atmosphere by the flamboyant and fun-loving Walter Hagen, the British contingent got far more than they bargained for. Upon arriving in New York, they were feted to official dinners, sporting events and cocktail parties far more lavish than they were accustomed to in Great Britain.

On June 3, 1927 the inaugural matches took place on a golf course designed by one of Britain's own, Donald Ross. Despite the rough travel and exhaustive entertainment, the British team fared well at the start, but eventually fell behind to their gracious hosts. The American team captained by Walter Hagen claimed the first official Ryder Cup victory, defeating the British professionals 9 to 2. The inaugural match in 1927 cemented Samuel Ryder's legacy in the game of golf. To a lesser degree he would also be remembered as a philanthropist and gentleman who saw golf as an opportunity for goodwill, friendship and influence.

If Samuel Ryder was the Ryder Cup's driving force in Britain, Walter Hagen deserves much credit in America. At the time, Hagen was at the peak of his playing career having won his fourth straight PGA Championship in 1927. He worked diligently with Ryder and the PGA of America at organizing itineraries and venues for the inaugural matches. The Playing Captain of the '27 team, this colorful and fierce competitor shared Ryder's enthusiasm and vision for international play.

The Formative Years

In 1929, the Americans set off to defend the Cup at Moortown Leeds in Yorkshire, England. The Moortown course was known for harsh, windy conditions forcing the Americans to play a much different game from that at home. Over 10,000 people flocked to Leeds to see the famous Americans in action. The highlight of the '29 Ryder Cup was the head to head duel between the respective Playing Captains, George Duncan and Walter Hagen. In advance of their match Duncan is said to have overheard Hagen guaranteeing a victory. Outraged, Duncan said, "This guy has never beaten me in a serious match and never will." Duncan took it to his American counterpart, whipping Hagen with a 10 and 8 match play victory. With great pride Samuel Ryder presented the treasured Cup bearing his name to the smiling British Captain. For Hagen, it was a bitter defeat. Nevertheless, he felt the British victory underscored the merits of the tournament to be carried on for years to come.

A proud Samuel Ryder presents the Cup to British Captain, George Duncan. A dejected Walter Hagen looks on (right)

1929 Ryder Cup Teams

USA - *Walter Hagen-Playing Captain, Johnny Golden, Gene Sarazen, Al Watrous, Johnny Farrell, Joe Turnesa, Leo Diegle, Bill Melhorn, Horton Smith, Ed Dudley*

Great Britain and Ireland - *George Duncan-Playing Captain, Aubrey Boomer, Archie Compston, Henry Cotton, Abe Mitchell, Fred Robson, Charles Whitcombe, Ernest Whitcombe, Percy Alliss, Stewart Burns*

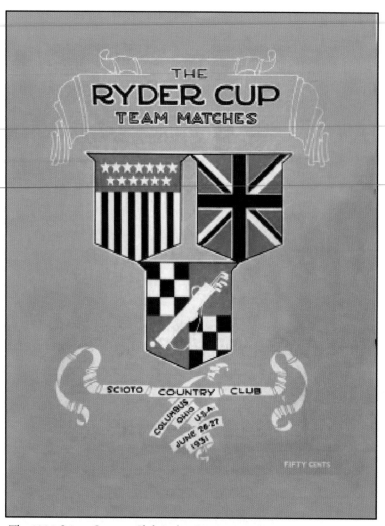

The 1931 Scioto Country Club Ryder Cup program cover

1931 Ryder Cup Teams

USA - *Walter Hagen-Playing Captain, Billy Burke, Wiffy Cox, Leo Diegle, Al Spinosa, Johnny Farrell, Gene Sarazen, Densmore Shute, Craig Wood*

Great Britain and Ireland - *Ernest Whitcombe-Playing Captain, Archie Compston, William Davies, George Duncan, Syd Easterbrook, Arthur Havers, Bert Hodson, Abe Mitchell, Fred Robson, Charles Whitcombe*

Walter Hagen's philosophy on who should play was a simple one -- if a player was good enough to be picked for a Ryder Cup team he should be a participant, not a spectator. Throughout Ryder Cup history, no player chosen for an American team has ever sat out of the competition.

The British team set sail in 1931 on the HMS Majestic for the third Ryder Cup Matches. On June 26th, play commenced at the Scioto Country Club in Columbus, Ohio, site of the 1926 US Open. Scioto was an excellent choice given that the US Open would be played a few hours away at the Inverness Club. Ohio's 100-degree heat stood in stark contrast to blustery conditions at Yorkshire. Once again at Scioto, Walter Hagen was the center of attention, not only for his play but renowned revelry. Legend has it Hagen brought a tray of cocktails to the first tee just prior to his match against British Captain, Ernest Whitcombe. Never one to turn down a drink, Hagen quickly put down a stiff one on the tee and then proceeded to nail his drive down the middle of the fairway. He later won a 4 and 3 victory that would contribute to a United States victory. Beyond the swagger and stellar play of their Captain, the United States assembled a team of far greater strength than the previous competition. The results played out accordingly with the USA whipping Britain 9 to 3.

In 1933, the Ryder Cup Matches were played at Southport and Ainsdale in Lancashire, England not far from its more famous neighbor, Royal Lytham. In an attempt to field a more formidable team Britain elected a Non-playing Captain who would select and prepare the players for competition. Their choice was J.H. Taylor, a member of the original 1927 team. Knowing the mental and physical strain that the Ryder Cup put on its participants, Taylor hired a team trainer who oversaw pre-dawn workouts on the beach in advance of the matches. Taylor's focus and disciplined approach paid off. The British team prevailed in a close match, 6 to 5, with Syd Esterbrook stealing the show on the final hole. The Prince of Wales presented the Cup to Taylor saying, "In giving this cup, I am naturally impartial. But, of course, we over here are very pleased to have won."

A pleased and proud Samuel Ryder had observed the matches overlooking the final green. It would be the last time he would witness the event that bears his name.

1933 Ryder Cup Teams

USA - *Walter Hagen-Playing Captain, Billy Burke, Leo Diegle, Ed Dudley, Olin Dutra, Paul Runyan, Gene Sarazen, Densmore Shute, Horton Smith, Craig Wood*

Great Britain and Ireland - *J.H. Taylor-Captain, Percy Alliss, William Davies, Syd Easterbrook, Arthur Havers, Arthur Lacey, Abe Mitchell, Alf Padgham, Alf Perry, Charles Whitcombe, Alan Dailey*

American Superiority Reigns

With the meetings all-square, the 1935 Ryder Cup Matches returned to U.S. soil at the Ridgewood Country Club in New Jersey. That year the Americans addressed Britain's concerns with the oppressive heat and decided that these and all future stateside matches would be played in the early fall. 1935 marked the final occasion that Walter Hagen appeared as Playing Captain. His Ryder Cup appearances were impressive to say the least and the '35 competition was no exception. Hagen went undefeated in foursome matches and lost only one singles match. The Americans would prevail and take the 1935 Ryder Cup. While the matches had been competitive to date, the edge was heading to the American's favor. They had far and away the best golfers in the world. It was an edge that would signal Unites States dominance for decades to come.

1935 Ryder Cup Teams

USA - *Walter Hagen-Playing Captain, Olin Dutra, Ky Lafoon, Sam Parks, Henry Picard, Johnny Revolta, Gene Sarazen, Horton Smith, Craig Wood*

Great Britain and Ireland - *Charles Whitcombe-Playing Captain, Percy Allis, Dick Burton, Jack Busson, William Busson, Ted Jarman, Alf Padgham, Alf Perry, Ernest Whitcombe, Reg Whitcombe*

The Ryder Cup Meets Trying Times

Samuel Ryder would not witness the tournament that bore his name in 1937. In December of 1936, Ryder suffered a massive stroke and died at the age of 77. Although his daughter, Joan, carried on the tradition of attending the Ryder Cup, its most ardent supporter would no longer be a part of its future. In '37, the rumblings of war were also being heard throughout Europe. A devastating World War would lead to a ten year hiatus before another cross-Atlantic competition took place, at least on an official basis.

A team was victorious on foreign soil for the first time in 1937. The Americans brought two promising rookies to Southport, Sam Snead and Byron Nelson, to challenge Britain's big guns, Henry Cotton and Dai Rees. The American's eventual 8-4 victory marked the onset of American's dominance and a drought for the British that would last for nearly 50 frustrating years.

The '37 matches also marked the end of Walter Hagen's legend and influence at the Ryder Cup.

He was one of the tournament's most colorful and dominant participants. Hagen's Ryder Cup legacy would include six stints as U.S. Captain, five as Playing Captain, four team victories, and a 7-1-1 record.

Samuel Ryder and daughter, Joan

The seventh Ryder Cup was to be played at the Ponte Vedra Club in Jacksonville Florida. In hopes that it would continue despite the pending war, the captains selected their team's rosters. It was not to be. The Second World War broke out in September of 1939. Any thoughts surrounding the next Ryder Cup were a distant consideration for anyone on either side of the Atlantic Ocean. Given that the Ryder Cup was still in its infancy, by many accounts, doubts remained about the future of the tournament.

"When we have settled our differences and peace reigns, we will see that our team comes across to remove the Ryder Cup from your safe keeping."
-- A message sent from the Secretary of the British PGA.

1937 Ryder Cup Teams

USA - *Walter Hagen-Captain, Ed Dudley, Ralph Guldhahl, Tony Manero, Byron Nelson, Henry Picard, Johnny Revolta, Gene Sarazen, Densmore Shute, Sam Snead*

Great Britain and Ireland - *Charles Whitcombe-Playing Captain, Percy Allis, Dick Burton, Henry Cotton, William Cox, Sam King, Arthur Lacey, Alf Padgham, Alf Perry, Dai Rees*

Hagen's 1937 winning team

Ryder Teams Benefit The Red Cross

The Red Cross Ryder team at Oakland Hills

The 1939 Ryder Cup team

With war devastating Great Britain any considerations about golf were tabled indefinitely. Many of those leading the sport in Britain were involved in the war, defending the very future of their country.

On the other side of the ocean, as America joined the fight, U.S. players organized a series of Ryder Cup exhibition matches to support the war as well as keep the spirit of the competition alive. Members of the United States team embarked upon a series of unofficial exhibition matches to raise proceeds for the Red Cross. One of these events, played from 1939 to 1943, took place at Oakland Hills Country Club.

Although the war ended in 1945, for the world and especially Britain, its devastating effects would remain for years to come. Shortly after the war's conclusion, the Ryder Cup encountered Robert Hudson. It is a little known fact that the Oregon fruit packer would be the person most responsible for the continuation and preservation of post-World War II Ryder Cup Matches.

The great Bobby Jones at one of the Red Cross Matches

Hudson Brings The Cup
Back From The Brink

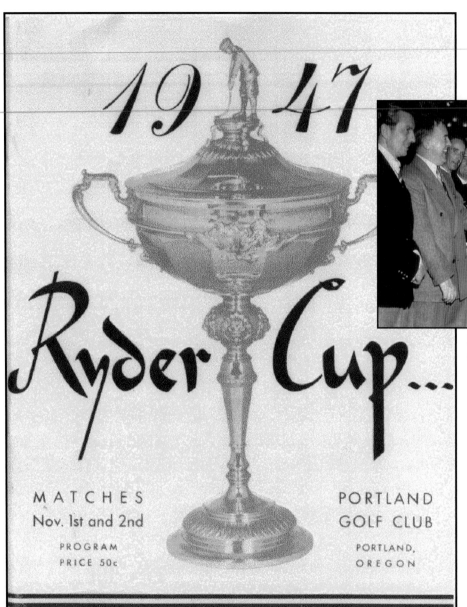

1947 Ryder Cup...

MATCHES
Nov. 1st and 2nd

PROGRAM
PRICE 50c

PORTLAND
GOLF CLUB

PORTLAND,
OREGON

The 1947 American team celebrates their victory

The 1947 Ryder Cup program

Robert Hudson's passion for golf equaled that of Samuel Ryder. Hudson served as a member of the PGA's Advisory Committee and petitioned to have the 1947 matches at the Portland Golf Club, his home course. Hudson offered to pay all expenses associated with the tournament. This genial and successful businessman single-handedly resurrected and saved the Ryder Cup Matches from extinction. Hudson carried on Ryder's vision of camaraderie and hospitality, greeting the British team as they arrived off the Queen Mary and hosting them for a lavish affair at the Waldorf Astoria Hotel in New York City.

1947 Ryder Cup Teams

USA - *Ben Hogan-Playing Captain, Captain-Herman Barron, Jimmy Demaret, E.J. "Dutch" Harrison, Herman Kaiser, Lloyd Mangrum, Byron Nelson, Ed "Porky" Oliver, Sam Snead, Lew Worsham*

Great Britain and Ireland - *Henry Cotton-Captain, Jimmy Adams, Fred Daly, Max Falkner, Sam King Arthur Lees, Dai Rees, Charlie Ward, Eric Green, Reg Horne*

Portland Golf Club's Robert Hudson

Of Robert Hudson, a member of the 1947 British team, Max Faulkner is quoted, "What he did was marvelous. Hudson did everything he could and would not accept a penny back, nothing more than a thank-you. We wouldn't be talking here about the Ryder Cup today if it wasn't for him." For more than a decade following the 1947 Ryder Cup Matches, Robert Hudson's largess continued for the American and British Ryder Cup players. At Christmas each were sent gift baskets compliments of this gentleman, another man who played a dedicated and important part of Ryder Cup history.

Ten years after the last Ryder Cup, play resumed in Portland, Oregon for the seventh time. Gone was the old guard led by Samuel Ryder, Walter Hagen and George Duncan. Playing Captain Ben Hogan, Sam Snead and Byron Nelson, as well as a talented roster of rookie players, led the new U.S. team. Henry Cotton and Dai Rees also brought a new crop of rookies, but so much like past, Britain was out manned and out played. They experienced their worst defeat ever losing to their hosts, 11-1.

Ben Hogan's thoughts on winning the Ryder Cup -

"We care about who is selected, but we care more about winning."

1949: Ganton Golf Club

A look at the Ganton golf course and clubhouse

The 1949 matches were played at the Ganton Golf Club in Yorkshire. The U.S. team arrived in England remarkably with Ben Hogan. Hogan had suffered a life threatening automobile accident just seven months prior, and to the amazement of all, was appointed as America's Captain. One of the Ryder Cup's first chapters in controversy played out at Ganton that year.

Having his integrity questioned in the '47 matches when he was accused of playing with illegal clubs, Hogan turned the tables on his rivals. The evening before the matches were to start Hogan petitioned to the Royal and Ancient Rules Committee that the British were set to play with illegal irons. His view turned out to be true and set a tone of ill will heading into the first day.

An assemblage of Ryder Cup greats from the WWII, Red Cross era

The '49 matches marked the second time Ben Hogan captained the U.S. team. To no one's surprise the discipline and tenacity he was known for on the golf course was reflected in the same manner he managed his team. The Americans emerged victorious 7-5 but dealt a far less humiliating defeat than what the British suffered in Portland.

1949 Ryder Cup Teams

USA - Ben Hogan-Captain, Skip Alexander, Jimmy Demaret, Bob Hamilton, Chick Harbert, Dutch Harrison, Clayton Haefner, Lloyd Mangrum, Sam Snead, Johnny Palmer

Great Britain and Ireland - Charlie Whitcombe-Captain, Jimmy Adams, Ken Bousfield, Dick Burton, Fred Daly, Max Falkner, Sam King, Arthur Lees, Dai Rees, Laurence Ayton, Charlie Ward

The Best Meet In Donald Ross' Backyard

Sam Snead, the United States Captain, proudly accepts the Cup from Joe Novak, President of the PGA of America.

President Eisenhower greeting contingents from the USA team.

The 1951 Ryder Cup Matches were played on one of the finest golf courses in the world, Pinehurst #2. This masterpiece is considered to be one of Donald Ross' greatest accomplishments. The '51 Ryder Cup presented the only occasion when the matches were not played on consecutive days. Play was suspended when the British players accepted an invitation to attend a University of North Carolina football game. The Americans declined to participate feeling that preparation and practice were far more important than a day on campus. When play resumed the British matched their hosts shot for shot early but putting problems resulted in yet another loss, thanks in part to Pinehurst #2's infamous greens. Hogan, back as a player, was replaced by Sam Snead as Playing Captain. Like his predecessors, Snead was fortunate to field another strong team that took care of business. The American's bested Great Britain 9 to 2.

From 1937 to 1953, United States Ryder Cup teams enjoyed the accompaniment of a team manager, the legendary Fred Corcoran. Along with his playing part in 1937 Ryder Cup competition, Fred will be remembered as one of golf's post-war pioneers. Throughout his career he served in various positions for the USGA, the PGA and LPGA, and in the process, led golf into its golden age. An astute businessman, Corcoran was one of the first sports agents, representing Tony Lema, Babe Zaharius and Sam Snead. Tribute to his dedication and accomplishments, Fred Corcoran was inducted into the World Golf Hall of Fame in 1975.

1951 Ryder Cup Teams

USA - Sam Snead-Playing Captain, Skip Alexander, Jack Burke Jr., Jimmy Demaret, Clayton Heafner, Ben Hogan, Lloyd Mangrum, Ed Oliver, Henry Ransom

Great Britain and Ireland - Arthur Lacy-Playing Captain, Jimmy Adams, Ken Bousfield, Fred Daly, Max Faulkner, Arthur Lees, John Patton, Dai Rees, Charlie Ward, Harry Weetman

Wentworth Golf Club, site of the unofficial matches in 1926, hosted British and American teams again for official play in 1953. To the surprise of many, the British team showed signs of promise. Two rookies, Peter Allis and Bernard Hunt, were primed to mount the best challenge the United States had seen in years. That year Ben Hogan and Dutch Harrison both declined to make the trip. One team's loss had been the other's gain. Henry Cotton, the European Non-Playing Captain, rallied his British team to one of the closest margins in Ryder Cup history. The matches went down to the wire with Allis and Hunt needing par for the win. Incredibly, both carded bogey sixes on the last hole and fell short of taking the championship. The hard fought matches ended at USA 6, Great Britain and Ireland 5.

The Wentworth Clubhouse

1953 Ryder Cup Teams

USA - *Lloyd Mangrum-Playing Captain, Jack Burke Jr., Walter Burkemo, Dave Douglas, Fred Hass Jr., Ted Kroll, Cary Middlecoff, Sam Snead, Ed Oliver, Jim Turnesa*

Great Britain and Ireland - *Henry Cotton-Captain, Jimmy Adams, Peter Allis, Harry Bradshaw, Eric Brown, Fred Daly, Max Faulkner, Bernard Hunt, John Panton, Dai Rees, Harry Weetman*

The PGA's Fred Corcoran (top left) with the 1953 United States Ryder Cup team

Tournament Time In The Desert

During Pre War engagements, travel could take up to four times longer than the matches themselves. That would change in 1955. With air travel emerging, the Ryder Cup was not relegated to East Coast venues thanks to new accessibility to the West.

For the 1955 matches, the two teams traveled to the Thunderbird Ranch and Country Club in Palm Springs, California. This was the first taste of desert golf for many European players. That year the British PGA unveiled a revision in the selection process, which favored a ranking system. A point system process now replaced their antiquated and subjective 'by-committee' method. No longer would players be selected at the pleasure of their team's captains.

Also for the first time players were allowed to choose which size ball to play, many opted for the smaller British ball on par fives. As always, the British team was more hopeful than confident heading into the matches. Dai Rees and Chick Harbert, both Playing Captains, mustered all they could from previous Ryder Cup experience. But once more, the results were still the same. The Americans again retained the Cup.

The USA team's victorious run was beginning to wear on the British contingent. Some suggested future matches be postponed until the British could assemble a competitive team. Although it was small consolation for the British, they accumulated the highest point total ever in a stateside match. Nonetheless, their losses were becoming all too predictable – United States: 8 and Great Britain: 4

1955 Ryder Cup Teams

USA - *Chick Harbert, Playing-Captain, Jerry Barber, Tommy Bolt, Jack Burke Jr., Doug Ford, Marty Furgol, Chandler Harper, Ted Kroll, Cary Middlecoff, Sam Snead*

Great Britain and Ireland - *Dai Rees-Playing Captain, Harry Bradshaw, Eric Brown, John Fallon, John Jacobs, Arthur Lees, Christy O'Connor Jr., Syd Scott, Harry Weetman, Ken Bousfield*

Lindrick Golf Club And Dai Rees' Revenge

Throughout Ryder Cup history match formats, qualification requirements and point totals continued to change, in most cases to make play more competitive. Unfortunately the results remained consistent until 1957. The American team's talent, depth, and strength remained insurmountable for Great Britain in spite of how hard they struggled to field a competitive team. Undaunted, the PGA of America and their British counterparts continued their biennial matches. Samuel Ryder's vision overcame many obstacles and carried on in the hopes for better days to come. For the British, the 1957 matches provided a tremendous boost and dose of confidence for Playing Captain Dai Rees and his team.

The '57 matches were the fifth appearance for Rees. The four previous losses were lessons in frustration for both he and his team. Rees was well acquainted with the Lindrick course, a short inland layout and controversial choice for host site.

That year the American team did not have the depth of experience and talent from previous years. Rees planned to use it to his advantage. As much as Rees knew of the Lindrick course, the opposite was the case for the visiting Americans. Jack Burke, the America's Captain, brought little experience to the table. The Americans came into the matches overconfident and were greeted not only by hostile competitors, but a feisty crowd as well. Upon finishing his final round, Tommy Bolt remarked, "They cheered when I missed a putt and sat on their hands when I hit a good shot." In the end, Dai Rees's strategy and experience trumped the American's overconfidence and complacency. For the first time in twenty years, the trophy would reside on British soil. It was sweet revenge. Great Britain and Ireland bested the USA, 7 to 4.

1957 Ryder Cup Teams

USA - *Playing Captain-Jack Burke Jr., Tommy Bolt, Dow Finsterwald, Doug Ford, Ed Furgol, Fred Hawkins, Lionel Hebert, Ted Kroll, Dick Mayer, Art Wall Jr.*

Great Britain and Ireland - *Dai Rees-Playing Captain, Peter Allis, Ken Bousfield, Harry Bradshaw, Eric Brown, Max Faulkner, Bernard Hunt, Peter Mills, Christy O'Connor, Sr., Harry Weetman*

Rough Travels And A Rough Reception

The PGA's Fred Corcoran with Bob Hope

Due to the PGA of America's qualification process some of golf's emerging superstars were unable to participate in the '59 Ryder Cup. Two notable names were Arnold Palmer who had won his first of four Masters Championships and Billy Casper, the reigning US Open Champion.

Sam Snead brought out some new and talented faces including Julius Boros, Cary Middlecoff and Mike Souchak, a former All-American college football player. Dai Rees' team consisted of virtually the same roster from two years prior.

From the onset the matches were another one-sided affair. The Southern California playground and desert lifestyle, although not highly regarded by golf purists, provided a glamorous backdrop and celebrity attendance with the likes of Bob Hope and Bing Crosby following the action.

Amid the glitter and opulence of Palm Desert, the Americans again decidedly bested their opponents 8 1/2 to 3 1/2. Following the '59 Ryder Cup, quiet discussions were under way to consider opening the selection process to players from the European Continent.

The trip to Palm Desert, California was the most trying part of Britain's 1957 title defense. After rough travel by sea that left many of the players seasick, the British contingent took a hair-raising flight to California that made its way through violent storms. Members of the team, along with their luggage, were thrown about the plane.

Upon arrival they were met by a new and more formidable American contingent. Playing Captain

1959 Ryder Cup Teams

USA - *Sam Snead-Playing Captain, Julius Boros, Doug Ford, Dow Finsterwald, Jay Hebert, Cary Middlecoff, Bob Rosburg, Mike Souchak, Art Wall Jr.*

Great Britain and Ireland - *Dai Rees-Playing Captain, Peter Allis, Ken Bousfield, Eric Brown, Norman Drew, Bernard Hunt, Christy O'Connor Sr., Dave Thomas, Harry Weetman, Peter Mills, John Panton*

European Futility Continues

The Royal Lytham and St. Annes clubhouse

October of '61 brought the Ryder Cup Matches back to Royal Lytham and St. Annes, and with them, another new format set forth by the British PGA. The British Committee moved to double the number of matches played and tournament points, somehow feeling that it would work to their advantage. Once again it would to be prove futile.

In '61, the American team added Arnold Palmer, Billy Casper and Gene Littler to their team's already superior roster. Their rookie counterparts on the British team proved to be no match. In route to victory, the Americans almost became the first winning team to leave without the Cup. In what turned out to be an awful embarrassment, Captain Jerry Barber realized he forgot to bring the trophy to London prior to the tournament. Fortunately a train trip to Northern England got the Cup to the matches in time to save Barber the humiliation.

1961 Ryder Cup Teams

USA - *Playing Captain-Jerry Barber, Billy Casper, Bill Collins, Dow Finsterwald, Doug Ford, Jay Herbert, Gene Littler, Arnold Palmer Mike Souchak, Art Wall Jr.*

Great Britain and Ireland - *Playing Captain- Dai Rees, Peter Allis, Ken Bousfield, Neil Coles, Tom Halliburton, Bernard Hunt, Ralph Moffitt, Christy O'Connor Sr., John Panton, Harry Weetman*

This new format, necessitating morning and afternoon matches, ended the player/captain role. "If the afternoon pairings are to be decided after the morning round it seems that a Non-playing Captain should be appointed. The strain of playing in the match, then spending one's lunchtime gathering information about the morning form, and making up one's team seem far too much to ask of any one player".
- Henry Longhurst, Sunday Times- London.

The General And His Army

The famous Arnold Palmer swing

instrumental in doing the same for the languishing Ryder Cup Matches. Thanks in part to Palmer's popularity, along with the new three-day format, the tournament generated substantial revenues and attendance of over 10,000 spectators in 1963.

The British again were no match for the American contingency. Some golf writers contended that the American team of 1963 was perhaps the strongest to appear in Ryder Cup competition. The Americans were again victorious in overwhelming fashion beating Great Britain and Ireland 23 - 9.

1963 Ryder Cup Teams

USA *- Arnold Palmer-Playing Captain, Julius Boros, Billy Casper, Dow Finsterwald, Bob Goalby, Tony Lema, Gene Littler, Billy Maxwell, Johnny Pott, Dave Ragan Jr.*

Great Britain and Ireland *- John Fallon–Captain, Peter Allis, Neil Coles, Tom Haliburton, Brian Huggert, Bernard Hunt, Geoff Hunt, Christy O'Connor Sr., Dave Thomas, Harry Weetman, George Will*

The East Lake Country Club in Atlanta, Georgia defined the dominance of not only the American team but also its last Playing Captain, Arnold Palmer. Palmer had won his second Masters in two years and successfully defended his British Open title at Troon.

With his stellar play and army of followers, Palmer became the center of the golf world. Not only did he revive the popularity of the British Open, he would be

> *"We know, and have known all along, since the game of golf got underway in America in the 1920's, that good players were in great numbers there. With the sun throughout the year, practice facilities and great rewards, we were up against an insoluble problem. The present top home players, by no means poor performers, are leagues outside the tough American ones."* **- Henry Cotton**

Royal Birkdale And Lord Byron

The Royal Birkdale Golf Club

The great Byron Nelson took the reins as Captain of the '65 Ryder Cup team. Since the inception of the matches, Nelson was the eighth man to lead an American team. Like his predecessors, Nelson fielded a talented lineup but one player etching his name into golf history was noticeably absent. Jack Nicklaus was the winner of a US Open, PGA Championship and two Masters Championships over three years. Nicklaus would have provided the Americans even greater horsepower, but he did not complete his PGA apprenticeship and therefore wasn't eligible for play.

Although the matches were not as unbalanced as in previous events the Americans took it to their opponents. Again calls went out to consider the inclusion of European Commonwealth players. So strong were the Americans, Nelson chose his top three players for the two singles rounds, Arnold Palmer, Julius Boros and Tony Lema, who proceeded to win six of six matches. The Americans once again retained the Cup with a 19 to 12 victory.

1965 Ryder Cup Teams

USA - Byron Nelson–Captain, Julius Boros, Billy Casper, Tommy Jacobs, Don January, Tony Lema, Gene Littler, Dave Marr, Ken Venturi, Arnold Palmer, Johnny Pott

Great Britain and Ireland - Harry Weetman-Captain, Peter Alliss, Peter Butler, Neil Coles, Jimmy Hitchcock, Bernard Hunt, Jimmy Martin, Christy O'Connor Sr., Lionel Platts, Dave Thomas, George Will

New Blood, Same Results

The 1967 US Team was one of the strongest team ever assembled in Ryder Cup play

1967 Ryder Cup Teams

USA - Ben Hogan-Captain, Julius Boros, Gay Brewer, Billy Casper, Gardener Dickinson, Al Gieberger, Gene Littler, Bobby Nichols, Arnold Palmer, Johnny Pott, Doug Sanders

Great Britain and Ireland - Dai Rees-Captain, Peter Alliss, Hugh Boyle, Neil Coles, Malcom Gregson, Brian Huggett, Bernard Hunt, Tony Jacklin, Christy O'Connor Sr., Dave Thomas, George Will

During the mid-1960s the smaller British ball was in use when the matches were played abroad. In 1967 Hogan chose to have it in play in Houston. One of the Ryder Cup's more humorous incidents took place between Hogan and one of the hottest players of the day, Arnold Palmer. On the use of the small ball;

Palmer: "Say Ben, is it right we're going to play the small ball? "

Hogan: "That's what I said!"

Palmer: "Well, supposing I haven't got any small balls?"

Hogan: "Who said you were playing?"

The 1967 Ryder Cup Matches traveled to the Champions Golf Club in Houston, Texas, one of America's great golf courses. The oppressive Texas heat forced the postponement until October. Ben Hogan returned as a Non–playing Captain and brought with him superstars like Gardener Dickinson, Bobby Nichols, Doug Sanders, current Masters Champion Gay Brewer, and Al Geiberger.

On the British side, Dai Rees came back as a Non-playing Captain with hopes to revive some of his past glory. The only newcomer of note was Tony Jacklin. Jack Nicklaus' poor showing at the Masters and overall point totals that year once again denied him a spot on the team.

Hogan pretty much summed up this chapter in Ryder Cup matches when he asked his team to rise at the opening ceremony and then said, " Ladies and gentlemen, the United States Ryder Cup team, the finest golfers in the world." It was far from an exaggeration. Sports agent Mark McCormick may have summed it up best saying, "Americans playing on their home ground are no more likely to lose to the British than Boston is likely to apologize for the tea party."

Hogan again infused focus and discipline into his team directing them to bed by 10:30 PM. He also made all calls on who would play and when. His focus and tenacity in managing his team played very well in the ultimate outcome. The Americans won handily, 23 to 8.

Gentleman Jack Makes His Mark

1969 Ryder Cup Teams

USA - Sam Snead-Captain, Tommy Aaron, Miller Barber, Frank Beard, Billy Casper, Dale Douglass, Raymond Floyd, Dave Hill, Gene Littler, Dan Sikes, Ken Still, Lee Trevino, Jack Nicklaus

Great Britain and Ireland - Eric Brown–Captain, Peter Allis, Brian Barnes, Maurice Bembridge, Peter Butler, Alex Caygill, Neil Coles, Bernard Gallacher, Brian Huggett, Bernard Hunt, Tony Jacklin, Christy O'Connor Sr., Peter Townsend

Captain Sam Snead (center) with his United States victors

Great Britain and Ireland Team, Captain Eric Brown (center)

In 1969 Jack Nicklaus finally made his Ryder Cup debut at Royal Birkdale. No player in Ryder Cup history would leave their mark as Nicklaus did during those matches. It was Nicklaus' show from start to finish. He won three matches and halved the fourth, the final with Tony Jacklin, Britain's emerging star and the reigning British Open Champion.

Going into the 18th hole, the match total was even with the Ryder Cup to be determined on the final hole of the all-important Jacklin/Nicklaus match. Having two-putted for his par Nicklaus watched as Tony Jacklin faced a three-foot putt to tie. Gentleman Jack chose to pick up Jacklin's ball mark conceding the putt, halving the match as well as the tournament. Nicklaus' sportsmanship would have done Samuel Ryder proud. The Americans and British battled to their first tie in Ryder Cup history.

Although the United States would officially retain the Cup, for the first time in almost 40 years, the Ryder Cup would be shared between the United States and Great Britain. There were mixed feelings regarding Nicklaus' sportsmanlike gesture on that 18th green. Some called it the most notable display of sportsmanship ever. Others like teammate Frank Beard and Captain Sam Snead were not as complimentary. Said Snead, "When it happened all the boys thought it was ridiculous to give him that putt. We went over there to win, not to be good ole boys. I never would have given a putt like that... except maybe to my brother."

*On the conceded putt: " I'm sure that's exactly what Samuel Ryder had in mind when he donated the Cup." - **Dave Marr***

Britain Faces The United States' Fearsome Foursome

lthough the American's dominance in Ryder Cup play would continue into the 1970's, the British team began to field a stronger contingent led by Peter Oosterhuis, Harry Bannerman and Brian Barnes. While their talent was formidable, Britain's new breed faced a fearsome foursome in Jack Nicklaus, Arnold Palmer, Lee Trevino and Billy Casper.

Old Warsom, a Robert Trent Jones course outside St. Louis, hosted the '71 matches. It was the longest Ryder Cup course of record at nearly 7,300 yards. For the first time in recent memory, the United States faced the real possibility of losing the Cup. Jack Nicklaus' concession to Tony Jacklin two years prior set the Americans up for a challenge they had not seen in years.

Jay Hebert, the United States' Captain, had little reason to doubt his team retaining the Cup. In addition to his feared foursome Hebert fielded a group of newcomers that included J.C. Snead, Dave Stockton, Charles Coody and Mason Rudolph.

The British team had their best start on American soil leading 3-1 in the early going. Some questionable decision-making by British Captain Eric Brown led to the erosion of his team's momentum. His team put a respectable fight, showing their best performance ever in the United States. It would not be enough. The home team dominated the four-ball matches in route to an 18 to 13 victory. With yet another loss the British team's frustration was reaching new heights. Tony Jacklin increasingly resented the unrealistic hopes presented about the British team's chances and lost much of the fire he brought to previous competitions.

1971 Ryder Cup Teams

USA - *Captain–Jay Hebert, Miller Barber, Frank Beard, Billy Casper, Charles Coody, Gardiner Dickinson, Gene Littler, Jack Nicklaus, Arnold Palmer, Mason Rudolph, J. C. Snead, Dave Stockton, Lee Trevino*

Great Britain and Ireland - *Eric Brown-Captain, Harry Bannerman, Brian Barnes, Maurice Bembridge, Peter Butler, Neil Coles, Bernard Gallacher, John Garner, Brian Huggett, Tony Jacklin, Christy O'Connor Sr., Peter Oosterhuis, Peter Townsend*

The Birthplace Of Golf Welcomes The Cup

Sunset at famed Muirfield

Prior to 1973, the Ryder Cup Matches held in Great Britain were hosted at golf courses located within England. This year the matches were moved to Muirfield in Gullane, Scotland. Muirfield, included in the British Open rotation, was regarded as one of the greatest links courses in the world. True to the character of most links layouts, the site posed a difficult yet fair challenge for both sides but gave the British a home-field advantage.

Jack Burke, leading the Americans that year, was the last losing U.S. Captain. This time around he brought with him a handful of impressive rookies including Tom Weiskopf, Homero Blancas, Chi Chi Rodriguez and Lou Graham. Team selection criteria though worked to America's disadvantage. Two of the game's rising stars, Lanny Wadkins and Johnny Miller, who carded a remarkable final round 63 at the US Open that year, were not eligible for play. The British Captain, Bernard Hunt, professed confidence leading to play in '73. He had doubts about the play of his competitors saying that they "hardly had a decent swing among them." Heading into the final stages of the competition, Hunt had reason for optimism. His team had a three-point lead fueling confidence that they could very well win the Cup. A tough blow reversed fortunes when Bernard Gallacher fell ill with a stomach virus and had to be replaced at the last minute by Peter Butler. Butler would be known as the first player to score a hole-in-one during Ryder Cup competition but would lose consecutive matches to American stars that included Nicklaus, Palmer, Weiskopf and J.C. Snead.

The win came as great relief to Jack Burke. Having been the last captain to lose the Ryder Cup, he remarked, "I didn't think I was going to get that one either – it looked like 0-2 to me." Although exonerated by captaining the winning team, Jack Burke replied to the question of returning to captain a third time saying, "Don't call me, I'll call you."

1973 Ryder Cup Teams

USA - Jack Burke Jr.-Captain, Tommy Aaron, Homero Blancas, Gay Brewer, Billy Casper, Lou Graham, Dave Hill, Jack Nicklaus, Arnold Palmer, Chi Chi Rodriguez, J.C. Snead, Lee Trevino, Tom Weiskopf

Great Britain and Ireland *- Bernard Hunt-Captain, Brian Barnes, Maurice Bembridge, Peter Butler, Clive Clark, Neil Coles, Bernard Gallacher, Brian Huggett, Tony Jacklin, Christy O'Connor, Sr., Peter Oosterhuis, Eddie Pollard, John Garner*

1975: Laurel Valley

The 1975 matches were held in Arnold Palmer's back yard at Laurel Valley, a course he represented as its touring professional. The consistent streak of U.S. victories made the Americans the presumed winner before the matches even began. On top of historical precedent at the Ryder Cup, American team members had dominated major championship play, having won the previous US Open, three British Opens and a host of PGA Championships. Despite a predictable outcome, the Ryder Cup typically provided a measure of surprise thanks to its match play format. The year at Laurel Valley was no exception.

Despite a commanding U.S. lead heading into final round play, the man many claimed to be the best player ever was defeated twice in singles matches by the same British opponent. The morning singles match between Jack Nicklaus and Brian Barnes went to Barnes 4 and 2. Palmer, knowing Nicklaus' surprised reaction, chose Jack for an encore afternoon match and hopeful retribution. Nicklaus was quoted as saying to Barnes in advance of the second meeting, "You beat me once, but I'll be dammed if you'll best me twice." Damned he was as the world's greatest fell again 2 and 1 to an elated Barnes. Despite the matches being so one sided, they continued to grow in popularity as a spectator sport in America. Over 21,000 attended the matches in 1975 and witnessed the ever-victorious Americans win by a margin of 21-11.

With America's continued dominance, coupled with a fast-developing European Tour, there was again increasing motivation to allow Continental European players into the competition.

1975 Ryder Cup Teams

USA - *Arnold Palmer-Captain, Billy Casper, Raymond Floyd, Al Geiberger, Lou Graham, Gene Littler, Hale Irwin, Johnny Miller, Bob Murphy, Jack Nicklaus, J.C. Snead, Lee Trevino, Tom Weiskopf*

Great Britain and Ireland - *Bernard Hunt-Captain, Brian Barnes, Maurice Bembridge, Eamonn Darcy, Bernard Gallacher, Tommy Horton, Brian Huggett, Guy Hunt, Tony Jacklin, Christy O'Connor, Jr., John O'Leary, Peter Oosterhuis, Norman Wood*

> "I still in all these years have difficulty in getting away from it. Whenever I attend a company day or dinner, I am introduced as the man who twice beat Jack Nicklaus head-to-head. I never consider it that fantastic. Certainly I enjoyed it at the time, but in my own mind I soon forgot it."
>
> **- Brian Barnes on defeating Jack Nicklaus.**

Jack Suggests A More Inclusive Cup

For those longing to level the playing field, the 1977 matches at Royal Lytham would edge toward much improved competition at the Ryder Cup. As always, the British team looked for signs of hope. This year's hope centered on a new arrival, Nick Faldo, who would later become one of the Ryder Cup's most storied champions. More importantly, the format of the matches was also altered. The changes resulted in

Jack Nicklaus and Tom Watson

fewer matches being played, giving some the belief that the British could seize an early lead and have a better chance of hanging on than in previous competitions. The new format did provide the British side with a chance heading into final round singles play. While ten matches presented opportunity, the American's five-point lead presented too great a challenge for their competitors to overcome. The Americans again won 12$^{1/2}$ to 7$^{1/2}$.

The American's victory marked a twenty-year drought for Great Britain, which had only won three matches dating back to 1927. One of the most important events ever to take place at the Ryder Cup happened that year at Royal Lytham when Jack Nicklaus approached the leadership of the American and British PGA with an informal suggestion to widen the scope of inclusion for European players. To Nicklaus, this was one of his most important contributions as a Ryder Cup participant. "When I'm asked what my favorite Ryder Cup moment is, it's funny I don't think of something that happened on the course," he said. "Making it more inclusive is my best Ryder Cup memory." After consulting with the Ryder family,

Lord Derby, President of the British PGA, opened the competition to qualifiers from countries beyond the boundaries of the British Commonwealth. This much anticipated and necessary change was precisely what the matches needed, not only assure their continuity, but to raise their level of competition, excitement and exposure.

With Derby's decision, European members of the British PGA and European Division Order of Merit would be included in the selection process. The timing for this move was excellent, given that the Continent was producing talented players anxious to compete with the ever-dominant United States PGA professionals. If the Americans had been looking for more competitive matches they certainly got their wish. 1977 would mark a new era in Ryder Cup Matches, but even then, nobody would anticipate the scope and magnitude in years to come.

1977 Ryder Cup Teams

USA - *Dow Finsterwald–Captain, Raymond Floyd, Lou Graham, Hubert Green, Dave Hill, Don January, Hale Irwin, Jerry McGee, Jack Nicklaus, Dave Stockton, Ed Sneed, Lanny Wadkins, Tom Watson*

Great Britain and Ireland - *Brian Huggett–Captain, Brian Barnes, Ken Brown, Howard Clark, Neil Coles, Eamonn Darcy, Peter Dawson, Nick Faldo, Bernard Gallacher, Tommy Horton, Tony Jacklin, Mark James, Peter Oosterhuis*

Not everyone shared the general enthusiasm of opening the matches to European players. "The very future of the Ryder Cup is again, and inevitably, raised. Should the team to face the Americans include other Nationals? To do so would spoil the traditions of the Cup and cause administration and selection headaches." - **Dudley Doust of the London Sunday Times**

Continental Europe Enters The Fray

Hale Irwin and Billy Casper proudly hold the Cup

The 1979 Ryder Cup Matches descended on the beautiful Greenbrier resort in White Sulfur Springs, West Virginia. New qualification guidelines opened Ryder Cup play to a crop of European players that year, including Seve Ballesteros who would go on to write his own chapters in Ryder Cup history. The '79 matches were also played during three days for the first time. The format, which is in place today, consisted of four foursomes and four ball matches the first two days and twelve singles matches on the final day. With this new format the number of points at stake was 28, as opposed to 20 the prior year at Royal Lytham.

The 1979 European Team

The 1979 USA Team

The new participants and new format did little to change the pattern that heavily favored the Americans. The U.S. team again prevailed, but nevertheless, would not look at their Ryder Cup competitors in the same manner again. "I didn't get a strong sense of the opposition being that much changed," recalled U.S. Captain, Billy Casper. "But we never took them for granted, and I wasn't going to as Captain."

Despite losing 17-11, the European team consoled itself with the fact that many matches went down to the wire. While the American side once again prevailed, the new additions from Europe were a clear indication that the competitive nature and excitement of future matches would escalate.

1979 Ryder Cup Teams

USA - Billy Casper-Captain, Andy Bean, Lee Elder, Hubert Green, Mark Hayes, Hale Irwin, Tom Kite, John Mahaffey, Gil Morgan, Larry Nelson, Lee Trevino, Lanny Wadkins, Fuzzy Zoeller

Europe - John Jacobs–Captain, Seve Ballesteros, Brian Barnes, Ken Brown, Nick Faldo, Bernhard Gallacher, Antonio Garrido, Tony Jacklin, Mark James, Michael King, Sandy Lyle, Peter Oosterhuis, Des Smyth

Controversy And Conflict Stifles The Europeans

Jerry Pate, Tom Watson and Ben Crenshaw watch the action at Walton Heath

Approaching the 1981 Ryder Cup, Seve Ballesteros was becoming the center of attention having won the 1980 Masters in dominant and dramatic fashion. While he was arguably one of the top two players in the world, the '81 matches would not include one of golf's brightest stars.

Ballesteros did not make the '81 team due to a controversial dispute centered on his lack of appearances in Europe. Because he played very little in Europe, he had not earned enough points to be selected to the team. On Ballesteros' omission Tony Jacklin said, "The decision about Seve, who was arguably the best player in the world at the time, was sheer insanity." Jacklin had a right to be mad himself. He was asked to join the British team as an "official," in a non-playing capacity to which he declined.

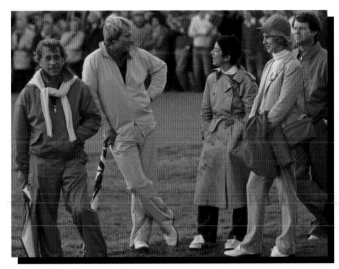

Left to right: Dave Marr, Jack Nicklaus, Mrs. Watson, Mrs. Nicklaus, Tom Watson

The American's selection process was far less controversial given that they would put the strongest team ever assembled into play at Walton Heath. Without a weak link on the team, the Americans represented a virtual who's who of modern day golf. Jack Nicklaus and Tom Watson headlined the team that included Larry Nelson, Bill Rodgers, Johnny Miller, Tom Kite, Bruce Lietzke, Ray Floyd, Jerry Pate and Lee Trevino.

Remarkably, Larry Nelson who was 5-0 in the previous Ryder Cup again managed to extend his undefeated record. He followed up his prior matches at Walton Heath by going 4-0. The American team lived up to its billing giving the Europeans a beating on British soil, 18 to 9. Although bringing contestants from Continental Europe into play for the '81 meeting did not bring about the desired results, the Ryder Cup Matches were playing to an audience ten-fold greater than before and earning significantly higher financial returns. Under the careful guidance of the PGA of America, the matches were beginning to develop into a more highly anticipated event.

The United States "one - two punch," Nicklaus and Watson

1981 Ryder Cup Teams

USA - Dave Marr-Captain, Ben Crenshaw, Hale Irwin Tom Kite, Raymond Floyd, Bruce Lietzke, Johnny Miller, Larry Nelson, Jack Nicklaus, Jerry Pate, Bill Rogers, Lee Trevino, Tom Watson

Europe - John Jacobs–Captain, Jose Maria Canizares, Howard Clark, Eamonn Darcy, Nick Faldo, Mark James, Bernard Gallacher, Bernhard Langer, Sandy Lyle, Peter Oosterhuis, Manuel Pinero, Des Smyth, Sam Torrance

The Competitive Fire Is Lit

1983 USA Ryder Team

The 1983 Ryder Cup Matches came to South Florida at the PGA National Resort and Spa. Two experienced Captains, Jack Nicklaus and Tony Jacklin, provided the necessary leadership and gamesmanship to inspire their troops.

> *"The ninety-five-degree heat, the Europeans won't be accustomed to that. The Bermuda grass, they won't know too much about that. Then there's the fact we win most of the time"*
> **- 1983 USA Captain- Jack Nicklaus**

With bitter feelings surrounding his '81 omission, Tony Jacklin had written off future participation in the Ryder Cup. In a sudden turn of events he was approached at a tournament in Leeds and asked to be the European Captain for the 1983 Ryder Cup. After much consideration Jacklin agreed, provided Europe would dramatically change its approach to the matches. He strongly felt their disorganized approach, coupled with second-class accommodations, fueled the inferiority complex that plagued his team for years.

In '83 Jacklin took a chapter out of Walter Hagen's play book treating all involved with the Ryder Cup to a first-class experience. Players and caddies traveled on the Concorde, stunning uniforms were worn throughout, and five-star accommodations underscored the Europeans' renewed focus and commitment to turn the tide.

Beyond better treatment for his team, Jacklin insisted that the Europeans field the best team the Continent could offer. Jacklin sold Seve Ballesteros on joining the team that would also include Nick Faldo, Bernhard Langer, Ian Woosnam and Sandy Lyle. With a strong nucleus, Jacklin arrived at Palm Beach Gardens with the Europeans' best team since World War II.

With six European countries represented in '83, Jacklin's troops brought with them a new psychological resolve. Heading into Sunday's final matches, the Americans were in the unfamiliar position of trailing their counterparts. That evening Nicklaus insisted on victory, telling his team, "I do not want to be remembered as the first Captain to lose on American soil."

The Sunday matches presented a terrific battle. In what proved to be one of the best shots in Ryder Cup history, Lanny Wadkins worked a 60-yard pitching wedge through the teeth of the wind that landed a foot from the pin on the 18th green. His birdie earned a half point against Jose Maria Canizares, helping the Americans seal a $14^{1/2}$ to $13^{1/2}$ victory.

The overall match results were one of the closest on record and signaled a major shift in mindset for the future. These '83 matches proved that a change in attitude would be important going forward, given the American team was now vulnerable on their home turf.

Including the European players proved beneficial that year, accounting for 9 of the $13^{1/2}$ point team total. With Tony Jacklin's inspirational leadership, these matches played a significant role in raising the bar for spirit and intensity.

The PGA of America, whose magnificent golf course played host to these closely contested matches, was eagerly anticipating the next meeting at the Belfry. It was becoming apparent that the Ryder Cup was no longer simply a meeting of players representing their respective countries for a few days of match play golf. The Ryder Cup was evolving into a major event the likes of which no one, including the PGA, had envisioned.

> "We will not be the favorites when we go to the Belfry in two years. This score was no joke."
>
> - 1983 USA Captain- Jack Nicklaus

1983 Ryder Cup Teams

USA - *Jack Nicklaus-Captain, Ben Crenshaw, Bob Gilder, Raymond Floyd, Jay Haas, Tom Kite, Gil Morgan, Calvin Peete, Craig Stadler, Curtis Strange, Lanny Wadkins, Tom Watson, Fuzzy Zoeller*

Europe - *Tony Jacklin-Captain, Seve Ballesteros, Gordon Brand Jr., Ken Brown, Jose Maria Canizares, Nick Faldo, Bernard Gallacher, Bernhard Langer, Sandy Lyle, Sam Torrance, Brian Waites, Paul Way, Ian Woosnam*

Europe Finally Turns The Tide

Tony Jacklin leads his European Team to victory

Commercial considerations led to the choice of The Belfry, located near Birmingham England, as host site for the '85 matches. In many ways, the Belfry was similar to golf courses found in the United States and was not the best choice of venues as far as Tony Jacklin was concerned. He would have preferred a links-style course and the challenging conditions they can bring to the table.

Nevertheless, Jacklin was as anxious as ever to take on the Americans and avenge Europe's loss at PGA National. For the first time in Ryder Cup history, the Europeans fielded a team with strength and depth comparable to their American rivals. More importantly, they had confidence in their chances for victory. Coming so close in 1983 gave the Europeans the experience and fierce determination needed to be champions.

With a newfound passion, thanks in large part to Seve Ballesteros, the Europeans led a major comeback after a slow start. In what was regarded as major turning point, Craig Stadler carelessly missed a 14-inch putt that would have given him a victory during a critical stage in the competition. Said Curtis Strange, "Every one of us has missed a putt of that length, more than once. But you do that in the Ryder Cup, and it stays with you forever." This critical miss gave the Europeans and their partisan crowd the belief that luck was finally on their side. The vast crowds cheered American misfortunes at every chance, causing Sam Torrance to remind the spectators that they "were not at a football match."

After decades of disappointment, the European team rode their new horses and a partisan crowd to a convincing victory. A proud Tony Jacklin celebrated an overwhelming victory and largest European margin in Ryder Cup history. The Europeans bested their opponents by a stunning 16 to 11 point total. Europe had finally come of age with a roster of superb and experienced players that would become future Ryder Cup legends, including Ian Woosnam, Seve Ballesteros, Sam Torrance, Nick Faldo and Bernhard Langer.

1985 Ryder Cup Teams

USA - *Lee Trevino-Captain, Raymond Floyd, Peter Jacobson, Hubert Green, Tom Kite, Andy North, Mark O'Meara, Calvin Peete, Craig Stadler, Curtis Strange, Hal Sutton, Lanny Wadkins, Fuzzy Zoeller*

Europe - *Tony Jacklin-Captain, Seve Ballesteros, Ken Brown, Jose Maria Canizares, Howard Clark, Nick Faldo, Bernhard Langer, Sandy Lyle, Manuel Pinero, Jose Rivero, Sam Torrance, Paul Way, Ian Woosnam*

"The foreign team challenged and won and turned indifference into international intrigue because of that freak batch of childbirths in a calendar's time. You know the one in 1957-58, when into the world came Seve Ballesteros, Nick Faldo, Bernhard Langer, Ian Woosnam and Sandy Lyle. It is a rare overnight harvest second only to the unthinkable offering of Hogan, Snead and Nelson."
- Jeff Rude, Golfweek

Jack Tastes Bitter Defeat At Muirfield Village

The European team was victorious in Jack's backyard.

Two men synonomous with Ryder Cup history, Jack Nicklaus and Tony Jacklin.

"We believe we can win on American soil for the first time. I have been coming to America for twenty years, and this is the first time I am really confident of winning."
-European Captain Tony Jacklin before the '85 matches began.

The '87 matches came to Muirfield Village in Dublin, Ohio. This spectacular layout, designed by Jack Nicklaus, was one of the finest ever to hold a Ryder Cup competition. To make it even more special, Nicklaus took the reins as Captain for the second time against his European counterpart Tony Jacklin.

Heading into the matches, the Americans would assume that past history would indicate a victory and return of the Ryder Cup to its rightful place. In reality, the Americans had never faced such a formidable challenge heading to Columbus, Ohio. The golf world had seen significant change overseas with some of the sport's best and most accomplished players coming from Britain and the European Continent. Coupled with a strong bench, intimidation that plagued the Europeans was gone. They played regularly at PGA Tour stops and knew their American counterparts better than at any time in history.

The competition began with the Ohio State marching band parading up the 18th fairway, followed by Jack Nicklaus declaring of his team, "I could not have 12 finer players, or 12 finer gentleman." His team consisted of six newcomers against a more seasoned European team. Nevertheless, few imagined that Jack Nicklaus would tolerate an American defeat on his home turf, at his own club.

Muirfield Village, site of the 1987 matches

Despite the Nicklaus' home field advantage, the Europeans surged in the first round of play, winning six of eight opening matches. The Europeans never looked back. When all was said and done they had beaten the American team, 15 to 13.

Jacklin's hard-nosed coaching paid off again in '87. By virtue of being have-nots in Ryder Cup play, the European players displayed an aggressive tenacity far greater than their American equivalents who were accustomed to living large on the PGA Tour.

Commenting on his team's second consecutive victory, Jacklin said, "It was probably the best week of my life."

Nicklaus was the first United States Captain to lose at home. Following the defeat he said, "Captaining a U.S. team to its first loss at home at Muirfield in 1987 has to be my Ryder Cup low. Looking back, I'm glad I was in that position, because I wouldn't have wanted anybody else to go through the criticism and anger and second-guessing that came after that match." He then added, "It was inevitable that a European victory in the United States would happen – but I would have preferred it to be another time."

For the first time the matches were given television coverage for all three days in the United States and throughout Europe. They were now enjoying newfound attention and prestige, with revenue from television broadcasts, greater attendance and corporate sponsorship interest.

As the Ryder Cup competition approached the 1990's, Samuel Ryder's brainchild began to take on a different personality. Thanks to heated competition and formidable talent on both sides of the Atlantic, the Ryder Cup began to find a deserving place along side the Masters, the US Open, British Open and PGA as one of golf's premier events.

The modern day Ryder Cup's prestige, visibility and global appeal had made it a must see event for millions of people. For those intending to see the matches up-close, admission became more difficult than any other tournament including the Masters. They also became a major source of revenue for host sites as well as the PGA of America.

1987 Ryder Cup Teams

USA - Jack Nicklaus–Captain, Andy Bean, Mark Calcavecchia, Ben Crenshaw, Tom Kite, Larry Mize, Larry Nelson, Dan Pohl, Scott Simpson, Payne Stewart, Curtis Strange, Hal Sutton, Lanny Wadkins

Europe - Tony Jacklin–Captain, Seve Ballesteros, Gordon Brand Jr., Ken Brown, Howard Clark, Eamonn Darcy, Nick Faldo, Bernhard Langer, Sandy Lyle, Jose Maria Olazabal, Jose Rivero, Sam Torrance, Ian Woosnam

Europe Establishes Modern Day Dominance

The Europeans celebrating the events at the Belfry in '89

For nearly sixty-years, the United States dominated Ryder Cup play. All told, they had lost five times, but included the previous two meetings. For the first time in history the United States team entered the matches clearly on the defensive.

Their Captain, the ever-competitive Raymond Floyd, was chosen to resurrect the sagging spirits of his American teammates. For Tony Jacklin, his quest as Captain was a simple one - retain the Cup, and in the process, establish European dominance for the first time in Ryder Cup history. To do so he had brought back much of the same team to the Belfry. Floyd added five rookies, including Paul Azinger, Chip Beck, Fred Couples, Ken Green and Mark McCumber. He clearly needed veteran strength with his captain's picks, choosing Lanny Wadkins and Tom Watson to round out his team.

The American team was subjected to a tough reception from the European spectators. Following the boisterous European celebration held at Muirfield Village, a record crowd showed up at the Belfry for the largest golf tournament ever held in Great Britain. For the first time, the Ryder Cup was a sold-out show.

Taking a page out of Ben Hogan's book, Ray Floyd introduced his team as "the twelve greatest players in the world." It didn't sit well with the Europeans, but they chose to let their play speak for itself.

The '89 matches were the closest ever. Heading down to the wire, Curtis Strange displayed amazing grit, carding birdies at the 15th, 16th and 17th holes to erase the lead held by Ian Woosnam. He then knocked his approach to eight feet on the 18th hole to win the match. This ultimately led to a 14-14 tie that kept the Cup in Europe's hands. In the process European Captain Tony Jacklin would be the first Captain to retain the trophy three consecutive times. Once accustomed to a virtual monopoly of Ryder Cup victories, the Americans saw the tables turned and would wait two more years before they could take another run on their home soil.

Seve Ballesteros and Jose Maria Olazabal feel the strain of Ryder Cup competition

1989 Ryder Cup Teams

USA - *Raymond Floyd–Captain, Paul Azinger, Chip Beck, Mark Calcavecchia, Fred Couples, Ken Green, Tom Kite, Mark McCumber, Mark O'Meara, Payne Stewart, Curtis Strange, Lanny Wadkins, Tom Watson*

Europe - *Tony Jacklin-Captain, Seve Ballesteros, Gordon Brand Jr., Howard Clark, Jose Canizares, Nick Faldo, Mark James, Bernhard Langer, Christy O'Connor, Jr., Ronan Rafferty, Jose Maria Olazabal, Sam Torrance, Ian Woosnam*

The War On The Shore

One of the Ryder Cup's more memorable moments: Bernard Langer's miss at #18

The Ryder Cup would be changed forever with the "War on the Shore." For the third consecutive time the United States team arrived with nagging memories of bitter defeat. The atmosphere at Kiawah took on a level of intensity never seen at a golf tournament of any kind. The United States had just concluded Operation Desert Storm, fueling patriotic fervor with both the players and spectators. Fans, sporting red, white and blue en masse, were boisterous and committed to giving the U.S. players the emotional support needed to win back the cup.

The feelings of ill will between the teams was visibly apparent, escalating to a new high when Seve Ballesteros accused Paul Azinger and Chip Beck of cheating during their opening foursomes march. The accusation was bogus, but left Azinger steaming with anger. Said Ballesteros, "The Americans have 11 nice guys…and Paul Azinger."

The American players celebrate with their fans

American Captain Dave Stockton had high hopes heading into play as did Europe's latest Captain, Bernard Gallacher. Stockton's woes began early when his rookie Steve Pate was injured in an automobile accident. Two other rookies, Corey Pavin and Wayne Levi, would join nine other American veterans pitted against the Europeans. By now the Sony World Rankings had become the global benchmark for player performance and statistics. Coming into Kiawah, the Europeans were measurably stronger and were well aware of it.

Play commenced at the Kiauah Island Ocean Course. The new Pete Dye layout at Kiawah had already laid claim to being one of his most difficult. Parallel to the Atlantic Ocean, its crosswinds and enormous waste areas presented challenges to the players on virtually every hole.

The Americans celebrate victory on the shore.

The matches were fierce, hard-fought battles from beginning to end. On day one, the American team was up one point. Day two, the overall score was tied at eight a side. The final round came down to the last match between Hale Irwin and Bernhard Langer, one of the most memorable ever played.

Coming back from one-down after 16 holes, Bernhard Langer pulled even when Irwin three putted the 17th. With matches all square coming to the 18th, a Langer victory would tie the overall match and give the Europeans the cup once again. Irwin would need a tie for the American's to win back the trophy. Irwin would miss his approach to the green, and eventually make a bogey five. Meanwhile Langer was on in regulation, leaving himself 30 feet to clinch the Ryder Cup victory. Facing excruciating pressure and a hostile crowd, Langer hit his first putt six feet by the hole. Stepping up to one of the most important putts in Ryder Cup history, Langer then missed his comeback. Both sides attempted to console Langer, for they all knew the devastation that would accompany a miss that significant. Said Ballesteros, "Nobody in the world could have made that putt. Nobody." To which Irwin added, "I would never, ever, ever, wish that last hole on anybody."

With this agonizing turn of events, the Americans landed a 14 to 13 victory and their first cup in six years.

The battle at Kiawah was a watershed event for the Ryder Cup and one for the ages. It presented a significant departure from the gentility of the players that competed in prior matches, exemplified by moments of open hostility and ultra-competitive gamesmanship. Intensity reigned at Kiawah. Competing for the Ryder Cup carried more meaning than ever before.

1991 Ryder Cup Teams

USA - *Dave Stockton-Captain, Paul Azinger, Chip Beck, Mark Calcavecchia, Fred Couples, Raymond Floyd, Hale Irwin, Wayne Levi, Mark O'Meara, Steve Pate, Corey Pavin, Payne Stewart, Lanny Wadkins*

Europe - *Bernard Gallacher–Captain, Seve Ballesteros, Paul Broadhurst, Nick Faldo, David Feherty, David Gilford, Mark James, Bernhard Langer, Colin Montgomerie, Steven Richardson, Jose Maria Olazabal, Sam Torrance, Ian Woosnam*

"The (three thousand) European fans, bless their smelly little underarms, actually issued a verbal challenge on Saturday when they began singing rowdy English football songs as they celebrated their team's amazing comeback. Our fans, bless their lemon-scented Evian breath, are still cheering and applauding as they do at a concert when they want Barry Manilow to sing "I write the songs" just one more time. We simply aren't accustomed to such raucous behavior on the hallowed grounds of a golf course, but it's time for a change."
- A humorous account from Ken Burger, Sunday Post Courier

Sportsmanship Returns To Ryder Cup Play At The Belfry

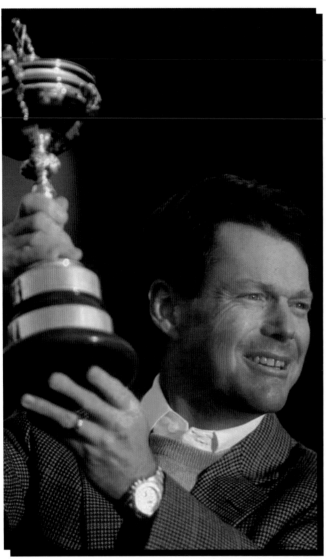

A proud Captain Tom Watson

Match play by its nature raises the competitive bar, but the Ryder Cup agenda sent the ploys, strategies and scheming to an even higher level. Tom Watson, the American's newly appointed Captain, didn't subscribe to hyper-competitive thinking, deferring to the goodwill and camaraderie of past Ryder Cup days. Unfortunately the Europeans did not share that same point of view. Decades of humiliating losses

and frustration gave them the resolve to have at it and even the score.

Setting a gentlemanly agenda turned out to be a difficult task, starting with his own team. Before Watson could get out of the U.S. he faced an embarrassing situation when a number of his players refused Bill Clinton's invitation to visit the White House. The issue was great fodder for the media, and the team was highly criticized before the matches even began. The players eventually agreed to make the visit, but the tone surrounding the team was not what Watson had in mind.

Before the first tee shot controversy also ensued as a result of Watson's regimented approach to the matches. This included the banning of all autographs until after the tournament. This well intended idea turned into a fiasco when he refused to sign Sam Torrance's menu at the opening dinner gala. The result was an angry British Captain and tabloids that were more than happy to paint another picture of the ugly Americans and their poor sportsmanship.

Fortunately, the following three days went on without incident and competitive sportsmanship prevailed. The '93 matches would be remembered as much for gentlemanly actions off the course as competitive play on it.

With Sam Torrance suffering from an infected toe, Tom Watson was forced to select a player to sit out in what would be an agonizing decision. Lanny Wadkins spared Watson the pain, opting out of

Sunday's action. "When I think about winning the Ryder Cup in '93, I think about how much Lanny's unselfish act contributed," Watson recalled. "It was for team and country."

That same night, European team member Peter Baker learned that his 11 year-old daughter had been rushed to the hospital with fears of spinal meningitis. The rules allowed that if a second player was unavailable, the other team could declare a forfeit and be awarded the point. In another act of sportsmanship, Ray Floyd declared that he would sit out if Baker was unable to play. The Americans refused to gain from the illness of a child. Davis Love III also sent a note on behalf of the U.S. team expressing concern for Baker's daughter. While Baker ended up playing Sunday, Bernard Gallacher pulled Love aside and thanked him for the note. Apparently these off-course incidents fell in line with Watson's gentlemanly approach after all.

On the course Watson's team stepped up their play during the final round singles matches that would determine the championship. Much of the attention focused on Love and Constantino Rocca. Heading into the 17th, Rocca had Love one-up, but would lose his lead by three-putting the hole. At the 18th hole, it appeared the pressure had gotten the best of both until Love stroked a six-footer into the center of the cup to win the match. Teammates and wives, certain that the win would lead to an American victory, mobbed Love. In one of the more memorable quotes on the intensity of Ryder Cup pressure, Love said afterwards, "I almost threw up on myself out there. I could not breathe, there was no saliva in my mouth."

Davis Love, (center), the man of the hour

Meanwhile, Ray Floyd was the other man of the hour making three birdies down the stretch to beat Jose Maria Olazabal 2-up to seal it for the Americans, 15-13. In his acceptance speech Watson said, "This is the finest moment I've had in the game of golf." It was a lofty statement considering Watson won five British Opens, two Masters and a heroic US Open.

1993 Ryder Cup Teams

USA - *Tom Watson-Captain, Paul Azinger, Chip Beck, John Cook, Fred Couples, Raymond Floyd, Jim Gallagher, Jr., Lee Jansen, Tom Kite, Davis Love lll, Corey Pavin, Payne Stewart, Lanny Wadkins*

Europe - *Bernard Gallagher–Captain, Peter Baker, Seve Ballesteros, Nick Faldo, Joakim Haeggman, Mark James, Barry Lane, Bernhard Langer, Colin Montgomerie, Jose Maria Olazabal, Constantino Rocca, Sam Torrance, Ian Woosnam*

"Under no circumstances did we lose the Ryder Cup. The Americans won the Ryder Cup. We tried our best. It's best not to think about the score line too much. I did not think anyone was to blame."
- European Captain Bernard Gallacher reflecting on his team's close fought match.

Anticipation Grips Oak Hill

The resolved European Team prevailed at Oak Hill

he previous two meetings gave way to the 1995 Ryder Cup Matches as being the most highly anticipated to date. For the media and Ryder Cup fans around the world, the Oak Hill matches would eclipse prior matches from virtually every perspective. The golf course, host to three US Opens and a PGA Championship, resembled an early June USGA layout complete with high rough, narrow fairways and lightening fast greens. The matches were close, competition intense and the Europeans resolve never greater.

As the event approached there was plenty of controversy surrounding the United States team, driven by a new rule that reduced the number of captain's picks from three to two. For the U.S.,

Lanny Wadkins' pick of Curtis Strange would backfire in the most visible way late Sunday. Strange hadn't won since the '89 U.S. Open, giving the belief to many in the press that Wadkins picked his friends instead of the best players at his disposal.

The opening matches brought wind and rain better suited for play in the British Isles versus Upstate New York. Combined with difficult course conditions and heavy rough, Oak Hill yielded high scoring and plenty of frustration on the first day. Heading down the stretch, the Americans came roaring back in singles play to position themselves for victory. The championship came down to the final match between Nick Faldo and Strange. Needing just a single par over the final three holes, Strange imploded under golf's brightest lights, making three consecutive bogeys. He lost the match, giving the Europeans their first Ryder Cup in six years 14 to 13. In winning the cup with a short putt, Faldo admitted to the unrelenting pressure. "It was horrible, everything was shaking but the putter," he said.

Strange, the controversial Captain's pick, went 0-3 in '95 Ryder Cup play and faced intense criticism from the golfing world following the match. Said Strange following the collapse, "I'm just disgusted with the way I played on the last two holes. I knew what would happen if I didn't perform as a Captain's selection. I'll deserve what I get in the press over the next few days."

Frustration loomed large for Curtis Strange, the controversial Captains' pick in '95

1995 Ryder Cup teams

USA - *Lanny Wadkins-Captain, Fred Couples, Ben Crenshaw, Brad Faxon, Jay Haas, Peter Jacobson, Tom Lehman, Davis Love lll, Jeff Maggert, Phil Mickelson, Loren Roberts, Curtis Strange, Corey Pavin*

Europe - *Bernard Gallacher–Captain, Seve Ballesteros, Howard Clark, Nick Faldo, David Gilford, Mark James, Per-Urik Johansson, Bernhard Langer, Colin Montgomerie, Constantino Rocca, Sam Torrance, Philip Walton, Ian Woosnam*

"America lost the Cup in a week Nick Faldo made two birdies, Seve Ballesteros hit three fairways, and the European captain forgot that Ian Woosnam existed. America lost the Cup with the number one player on the PGA money list, Lee Janzen, sitting on his couch at home…. America lost the Ryder Cup…. in the greatest come-from-ahead pratfall since DEWEY DEFEATS TRUMAN".

- Rick Reilly, Sports Illustrated

Drama At Valderrama

The Ryder Cup is played on the European Continent for the first time at Valderrama

In 1997, the Ryder Cup Matches were contested for the first time on the European Continent at the Valderrama Golf Club in Southern Spain. Valderrama, adjacent to the Mediterranean coast, is considered one of Europe's most difficult layouts. From start to finish, Seve Ballesteros stole the show. As a reluctant Non-playing Captain, Ballesteros put in motion the best strategies for the '97 matches since Dai Reese at Lindrick in 1957. The course, which Seve knew like the back of his

A jubilant Seve Ballesteros hoists the Cup.

hand, was set up to challenge the American players in every possible way. If the visitors were to retain the Cup, they needed to do so on golf course that Ballesteros personally masterminded.

Ballesteros also left his mark with a controversial decision for his second Captain's pick that some viewed as unethical. Ballesteros wanted Jose Maria Olazabal desperately to play on his team. Sensing an opportunity brought about by injury, Ballesteros demanded that Miguel Angel Martin take a fitness test to see if he was ready for Ryder Cup play. Martin had surgery on his hand, but it healed well enough for him to make a go of it. When Martin refused Seve's test, Ballesteros booted him from the team in favor of Olazabal.

Coming into the matches, the American team had no such controversy. They were loaded with talent, and by consensus, the overwhelming favorite to win. Given the results of the recent meetings, anything and everything could happen. And did.

It was all Seve's show in '97

Ballesteros' first target for gamesmanship was Tiger Woods, the reigning Masters champion. Seve boasted that any of his players could play against and beat Woods. Ballesteros and Colin Montgomerie then piled on Brad Faxon, insisting that he would be a non-factor due to his pending divorce. While the American's resented the remarks about Faxon and other U.S. players, they deferred in making the '97 Ryder Cup a war of words.

Ballesteros' course set-up also drew ire from the Americans, as alterations were made to neutralize their big hitters.

Highlighting the Ryder Cup's appeal, celebrities began to follow the events in Spain, with the likes of President George Bush, Prince Andrew and basketball superstar Michael Jordan in attendance.

The United States Captain was Tom Kite, a veteran Ryder Cup player, who assessed his team as "relaxed as any prior team going into the event." The Americans played like it in early action coming out of the blocks slowly. After the conclusion of the first day they trailed 4 to 3. After day two, the favorites fell even further behind and faced a five-point deficit.

Heading into Sunday, the pressure-packed environment once again consumed the world's very best. In advance of Sunday's singles match Tiger Woods said, "I'm feeling a lot of pressure. I felt it on the first day. I felt it on the second and now the third day." To which his coach, Butch Harmon, added, "Tiger told me he has never been so nervous in his life."

The Americans had to win all three of the four final day singles matches to win the cup. The stunned favorites went into Sunday play resolved to pull off the impossible – and almost did. But heroics from Bernhard Langer and Colin Montgomery sealed the deal for the Europeans, 14 to 13. Ballesteros experienced victory that required every bit of the strategy and gamesmanship he brought to the table. "It is very special playing the Ryder Cup in Spain for the first time and being Captain," said Ballesteros. "I've won a lot of matches around the world but there is nothing like the Ryder Cup."

1997 Ryder Cup Teams

USA - *Tom Kite-Captain, Fred Couples, Brad Faxon, Jim Furyk, Scott Hoch, Lee Janzen, Tom Lehman, Justin Leonard, Davis Love lll, Jeff Maggert, Phil Mickelson, Mark O'Meara, Tiger Woods*

Europe - *Seve Ballesteros-Captain, Thomas Bjorn, Darren Clarke, Nick Faldo, Ignacio Garrido, Per-Urik Johanson, Bernhard Langer, Colin Montgomerie, Jose Maria Olazabal, Jesper Parnevik, Constantino Rocca, Lee Westwood, Ian Woosnam*

Texas Governor George W. Bush gave American players an impressive inspirational speech prior to the final matches. Inspire the players he did, some even choking back tears, but by then, the deficit facing them had all but sealed their fate.

Combat Time At The Country Club

An ecstatic Justin Leonard after watching his 45' foot putt drop

The 1999 matches would raise Ryder Cup intensity to a full boil following an inconceivable conclusion to this event. The United States players had ample time to reflect not only on a humiliating defeat but the fact they lost the previous two Ryder Cups by a total of two points. With previous matches decided by razor-thin margins, it was becoming clearly evident that intangibles meant as much as talent in Ryder Cup play. The clear advantage from that perspective went to the Europeans. Many believed the European team of 1997 in particular, fueled by Seve Ballesteros, had more passion, more heart, and more desire to win than the Americans.

Captain Courageous Ben Crenshaw

A different mindset overtook the American team. Understanding the will and passion of their European counterparts, the responsibility for raising the emotional stakes rested with their latest Captain, Ben Crenshaw.

While mentally prepared heading into the play the American's fell behind quickly, trailing the Europeans 6–2 after the first round followed by a second day margin of 10-6. Ben Crenshaw, however, wasn't giving up. "I'm a big believer in fate," he said Saturday night. "I have a good feeling about this. That's all I'm going to tell you."

Heading into the final round the crowd became a bigger factor than ever before. Animated chants of

"U-S-A, U-S-A" continued throughout the day growing louder with each American win. It became a significant distraction. Numerous times players such as Colin Montgomerie and Jose Maria Olazabal had to back away from putts because of the raucous crowd noise.

Whatever magic Ben Crenshaw concocted began to fall into place on Sunday. Crenshaw, knowing the importance of a fast start, sent his top six players out early. It paid off in a big way. Hal Sutton, Phil Mickelson, Davis Love, Tiger Woods and David Duval all won their matches and set the stage for a classic finish.

A jubilant Hal Sutton

Two years of anticipation culminated with Justin Leonard's match at the 17th green. Leonard, without a win to his credit, trailed Ryder stalwart Jose Maria Olazabal by four shots with six holes remaining. He was clearly the underdog, criticized to the point that NBC analyst Johnny Miller said previously, "He'd be better off leaving and watching it on TV."

Leonard reeled off an incredible par-par-birdie-birdie run to win four straight holes and square the match coming to No. 17. His run included a 35-foot birdie putt on the 15th.

On the 17th, it became pure pandmonium. With both players on in regulation, Leonard faced a 45-foot putt for birdie. Olazabal had about 20 feet for his birdie three. Leonard, with little chance to sink the putt, simply tried to knock it close. As his putt popped off the back of the cup and dropped into the hole, it became the shot heard around the world.

Players, wives, caddies and PGA officials stormed the green to congratulate Leonard. It was in many eyes a deplorable act of sportsmanship. Olazabal had yet to attempt a makable putt to halve the hole.

If Olazabal were to make the putt the match would continue all square. Once order was restored, Olazabal made his run, but missed the hole by inches.

At the 17th and beyond, the Europeans had been subjected to questionable behavior from the American fans. Some likened Brookline to a "bear pit." The taunting of Colin Montgomerie was so bad that his father left the course, unable to tolerate the abuse. Following the matches, Mark James went so far as to say European golfers would refuse to play in future matches because of the attacks directed at his players. "A lot of players will not be bothered competing in American again," James said. "Certainly that is the case with me. It's not something I would look forward to. We don't need to be treated like this."

The Americans won back the Cup and showed the world that they had both the talent and intangibles to rise to the occasion. Unfortunately victory was earned under a dark cloud of questionable fan behavior, dubious sportsmanship and controversy. Many criticized the Americans' behavior at the 17th green as being contrary to the spirit of golf and the traditions attached to the Ryder Cup. Much was chronicled about that September afternoon when the outstanding play was overshadowed by controversy and hostility. Many questioned whether the win at all costs attitude had gone too far. Clearly events surrounding the United States' win were far from what Samuel Ryder had in mind in 1927.

1999 Ryder Cup Teams

USA - Captain-Ben Crenshaw, Jim Furyk, Tom Lehman, Hal Sutton, Phil Mickelson, Davis Love lll, David Duval, Tiger Woods, Mark O'Meara, Justin Leonard, Jeff Maggert, Payne Stewart, Steve Pate

Europe - Captain-Mark James, Darren Clarke, Paul Lawerie, Colin Montgomerie, Jesper Parnevik, Padraig Harrington, Lee Westwood, Jean Van de Velde, Andrew Coltart, Jarmo Sandelin, Sergio Garcia, Miguel Angel Jimenez, Jose Maria Olazabal

Among the scores of commentaries surrounding the unfortunate circumstances at the Country Club at Brookline, one stood out the most due to where it originated and whose comments were quoted. "It went way beyond the decency you associate with proper golf. I love the Ryder Cup and I don't want to see it degenerate into a mob demonstration every time we play it", Michael Bonallack, Secretary of the Royal and Ancient Golf Club of St. Andrews, the birthplace of golf and steward of its beloved traditions.

Risk Brings Reward At The Belfry

Sam Torrance celebrates another European victory

The overstated exuberance surrounding the Ryder Cup was diminished by the horrific and startling events of September 11th. The 2001 Ryder Cup Matches were postponed to 2002.

The Battle at Belfry may be remembered more for the Captains than the competition on the course. With the decision to keep 2001 teams in tact, regardless of the current year's rankings, both teams approached the Belfry without their very best players. The underrated European team set out to avenge their bitter loss at Brookline with a group of lesser-known players. These underdogs, in particular Phillip Price and Paul McGinley, shocked the United States team by beating them at their own game – the singles matches.

Going into single's play the matches were tied at eight a side. Curtis Strange held Tiger Woods, Phil Mickelson and Davis Love III back, electing to play them later in the line up. In theory it was practical decision. Sam Torrance, a playing hero in previous meetings, did the opposite, sending out his big guns at the beginning with astounding results. They won early and won big. Said Colin Montgomerie, "It was a huge risk. And it worked very, very well."

The conclusion of the matches occurred in stunning fashion. Rookie Paul McGinley made an eight-foot putt to halve the hole with Jim Furyk, giving Europe

Colin Montgomerie hoists the cup. He went unbeaten in five matches

the necessary 14 points to win the Cup. On his ill-fated strategy Strange said, "He (Torrance) took a hell of gamble by front loading his team like he did. Because if they don't do well, in my mind it's over." Following the matches, Strange conceded, "Sam snookered me out there. They did what they had to do and went off and got a lot of blue on the board."

For Colin Montgomerie, the 2002 matches were his finest hour. He was unbeaten in five matches. Incredibly, he never trailed in the 82 holes he played. Montgomerie and his teammates joined more than 30,000 fans that stuck around, singing, chanting and celebrating in the dark.

2002 Ryder Cup Teams

USA - *Curtis Strange-Captain, Paul Azinger, Mark Calcaveccia, Stewart Cink, David Duval, Jim Furyk, Scott Hoch, Davis Love III, Phil Mickelson, Hal Sutton, David Toms, Scott Verplank*

Europe - *Sam Torrance-Captain, Thomas Bjorn, Darren Clarke, Niclas Fasth, Pierre Fulke, Sergio Garcia, Padraig Harrington, Bernhard Langer, Paul McGinley, Colin Montgomerie, Jesper Parnevik, Phillip Price, Lee Westwood*

The Monster

AN UP CLOSE AND PERSONAL VIEW
OF THE OAKLAND HILLS SOUTH COURSE

A GLIMPSE AT THE MONSTER CHALLENGE

The Oakland Hills South Course is a combination of Donald Ross' design mastery and Robert Trent Jones' diabolical genius. While its reputation borders on the brutal, the South Course is a classic American venue for championship play and a fair test of golf. The course maintains an expansive, open layout. There are no blind shots. No "trick" holes. The critical factor, which will come into play throughout the Ryder Cup Matches, will be putting on the South Course's large, complex greens.

Many have described the Monster as a links-style golf course. Its wide, rolling fairways welcome players to go with their drivers. However scores of deep, well placed bunkers await nearly every tee shot. Except for the 5th, 7th, and the signature 16th hole, water hazards are few and trees are abundant.

At times, players can lose touch with the mystique of the Monster. For the Ryder Cup participants, this golf course will be a relentless test that offers a high degree of risk-reward opportunities from beginning to end of every match.

During past Ryder Cup Matches, Captains have influenced course set-ups to favor the play of their home teams. Generally this proved to be insignificant at impacting the final outcome with the exception of two cases, Lindrick in 1957 and Valderrama in 1999. In both cases the Europeans emerged victorious.

For 2004 matches, Oakland Hills' setup was to be impacted through the recommendations of Hal Sutton, the United States Captain. In advance interviews with the press, Sutton has indicated he will defer the setup to the PGA, recommending that it play similar to PGA Championship conditions.

The following pages offer an up close and personal look at 18 of the world's finest golf holes. Accompanying this view of the Oakland Hills South Course are some of the trials, tribulations and glorious moments experienced by some of the greatest names in golf during past major championships staged at the Club.

Number One
435 Yard Par Four

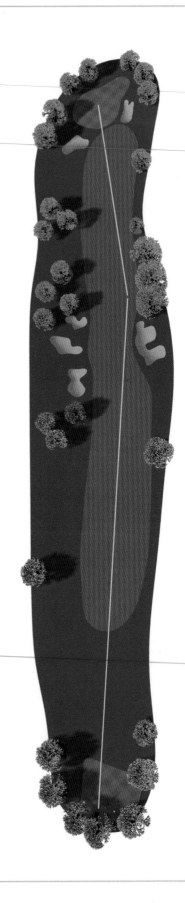

This excellent starting hole begins from an elevated tee and a narrow landing area guarded by fairway bunkers on both sides. A short-to-mid iron approach shot is critical to an undulating green where pin positions will determine the likelihood for birdie. The more difficult positions are left front which is guarded by bunkers and right back, where going over the green poses a difficult chip coming back. Again, pin positions will determine the outcome on this opening hole. It will be just the beginning salvo of many challenging approach shots to the Monster's intricate greens.

Walter Hagen, Oakland Hills' first golf professional, set up the Club's humble pro shop in a re-claimed chicken coop that stood beside the first fairway.

Number Two
527 Yard Par Five

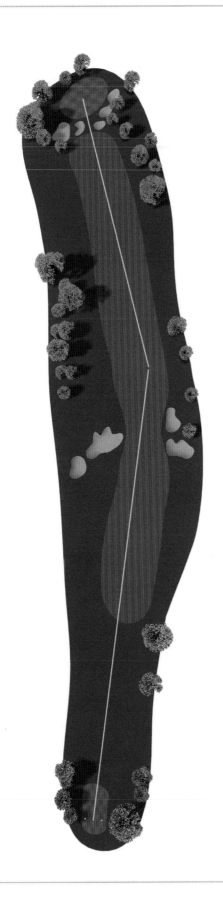

This reachable par five is a slight dogleg to the left that will accomodate an iron approach shot to a green sloping from back to front. Greenside traps and trees will catch an errant shot on the right making getting down in two nearly impossible. If the pin is back left and an approach shot does not hold the green it will roll down into a small collection area behind the green and make the shot coming back even more difficult due to the greens sloping away from the player. This is the first of only two par fives awaiting the participants.

During the first round of the 1985 US Open, a virtually unknown Taiwanese professional, T. C. Chen, accomplished one of golf's rare feats. He holed his second shot on this par five for the rarest of rare, a double eagle-two. It was probably the only time this occurred in Oakland Hills' eighty-year history.

Number Three
199 Yard Par Three

*B*unkers, the most dangerous of which are at the left front of this green, surround this par three. When the pin is positioned at the back left, these bunkers are most definitely in play. The green has less undulation than most. However there is just enough subtlety, depending on the pin position, to make par a good score.

Prior to the '91 Senior Open, Jack Nicklaus, in a practice round with friends, hit separate shots to each of the four quadrants of this green, predicting where the pin placements would be throughout the tournament. He was correct on all accounts and on Sunday the pin was, as expected, back left.

The 1979 PGA Championship resulted in a three-hole playoff between Ben Crenshaw and David Graham. Their putting duel climaxed when Graham made a clutch birdie two on this hole to win the championship.

Number Four
433 Yard Par Four

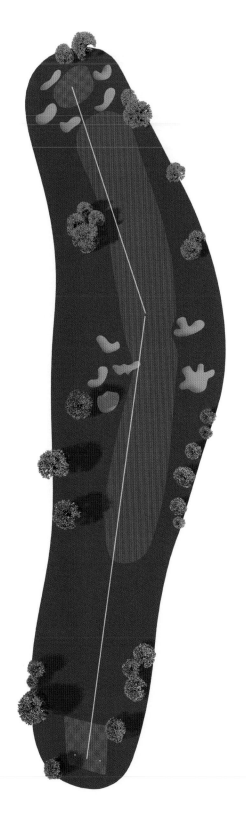

There is just enough trouble on this hole to make par an acceptable number. The landing area is narrow, with trees and bunkers on the left presenting a formidable challenge coming off the tee. For those hoping to cut the dogleg the risk is high but the reward will be a short downhill approach to an accessible green. The putting surface, sloping back to front is one of few on the course that allow straight putts and realistic runs at birdie.

At the 1991 US Senior Open, Arnold Palmer, hit his second shot right of the green into a drop area. After being denied relief from an official, Palmer played his shot to the green, took a double bogey and went on to miss the cut. When asked if a questionable call caused him to miss out on weekend play Palmer replied, "No, bad golf made me miss the cut!"

Number Five
457 Yard Par Four

This very difficult hole provides a challenging test from tee to green. The hole features a narrow landing area, countless trees on the left, bunkers on the right and a creek that is reachable from the tee. The green has more undulations and elevations than any other on the course. Bunkers guard the left, right and front of this putting surface. A player whose approach shot misses this green will be looking at a bogey or worse. So severe are the undulations on this green, there is virtually no location that gives way to a flat putt.

The old adage, "The Lord giveth and the Lord taketh" deftly applied to T. C. Chen's experience at the 1985 US Open. The same player who double eagled the second hole on the first day of play managed another rarity during the final round on Sunday afternoon. While enjoying a four stroke lead, the heavy rough caused him to double hit a greenside chip that eventually led to a quadruple bogey eight that erased his lead. Chen eventually lost the '85 Open Championship to Andy North by one stroke.

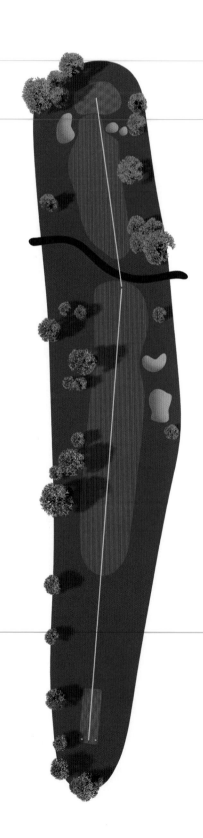

Number Six
305 Yard Par Four

This par four, the shortest on the golf course, has been modified for the Ryder Cup matches. The relocated tee box will allow the players to go for the green with a driver or fairway wood. In doing so they will be hitting to one of the Monster's deepest greens. Although it may be accessible to some tee shots, this elevated green is well-bunkered, contoured and sloped from back to front. Nearly every putt will break in either direction depending on the pin location.

Number Seven
405 Yard Par Four

Players coming off the seventh tee must navigate three bunkers on the left and a sloping fairway that tilts down to a small pond to the right. Although players may opt for a fairway wood or long iron, laying up will require an accurately played second shot to a narrow green. An errant shot will find bunkers on both sides which won't leave much green to work with. The putting surface slopes subtly from back to front. This seventh green has fewer contours than most but its subtle breaks make for a "get out of town" par.

Ben Hogan's first birdie during his final round at the 1951 US Open came at this seventh hole. It led to an eventual 67, which won him the tournament. His play on the final day is considered by many to be the best round played in US Open history.

Number Eight
450 Yard Par Four

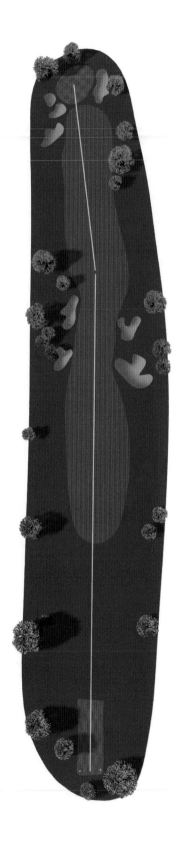

*P*layed as a par five for Oakland Hills' members, the eighth will be a long par four for Ryder Cup contestants. A narrow landing area flanked by bunkers on both sides will greet the players. The left bunkers are deep enough to force a lay up for the second shot. To reach the green in regulation, a long iron will be the club of choice playing to an elevated green. Guarded by bunkers on both sides, this contoured green slopes from back to front. To have the best chance at a tough birdie or respectable par, it is best to be putting from below the hole.

In 1985, Denis Watson's time literally ran out in his quest for an unthinkable US Open Championship, thanks in part to a penalty assessed on the eighth green. Watson waited too long as his birdie putt hung on the lip of the hole, eventually leading to a two shot penalty. Watson later missed the playoff and a shot at the championship by one stroke.

Number Nine
217 Yard Par Three

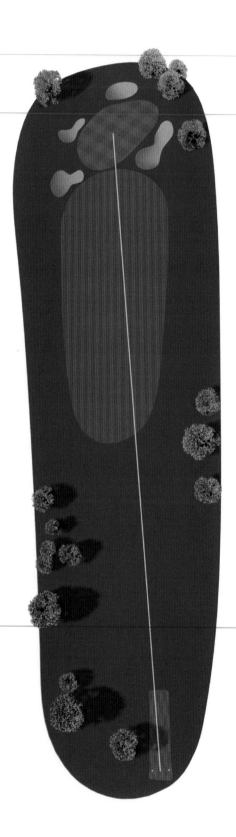

This is the second of four excellent par threes on the South Course. Its undulating green is one of the most difficult. There is a crown in the middle of the green and an elevated terrace on the left side, which will invite an interesting pin placement and make a birdie two a virtual miracle. There may be more three putts on this hole than any other throughout the matches.

In the 1979 PGA Championship, Ben Crenshaw had his way with the par threes at Oakland Hills. During the second round he hit a three-wood into the cup at the ninth for an ace. In the final round he made birdies at holes 3, 9 and 13. Had he continued his domination of the par threes with another birdie at 17, history would reveal a different story. He ultimately lost in a playoff to David Graham, ironically on the Par 3, third hole.

Number Ten
454 Yard Par Four

Players may opt for a fairway wood from this elevated tee. Three bunkers guarding the landing area will easily turn a potential birdie into at least a bogey. Beyond the landing area, this fairway slopes severely to the right and will take a drive from the middle of the fairway and feed it into the right rough. An uphill second shot takes a player to a green guarded with bunkers on both sides. This rather large, flat green has a slight ridge in the center. This 10th green is one of few that can easily accommodate a two-putt par.

At the 1924 US Open, defending Champion Bobby Jones, gave up six strokes to par on this hole during the four rounds of the tournament. He finished runner up to Cyril Walker by three shots. It can be assumed that had it not been for his misfortunes on this hole Jones would have successfully defended his 1923 championship.

At the 1951 US Open, Ben Hogan hit what he considered, one of the best shots of his career. Hogan struck a three-iron to within five-feet from the pin to birdie the hole and carried on to win the championship.

Number Eleven
411 Yard Par Four

There is little room for error on this very interesting par four. The fairway adjacent to the bunkers on the right provides an excellent landing area. A mid-to-short iron approach shot takes the player to a deep, narrow green which is easily four to five feet higher in the back than the front. Cavernous bunkers guard both front and sides of this green. Any down hill putt will easily slide past the hole, and if the pin placement is at the front, even off of the green.

Number Twelve
560 Yard Par Five

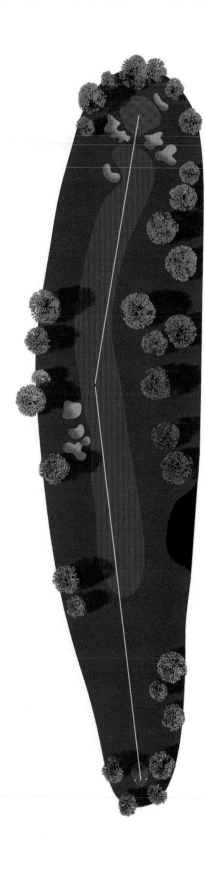

The longest hole on the golf course starts out from a tee box almost forty feet above the fairway. A very slight dogleg to the right, this hole offers tree trouble on the right and fairway bunkers to the left. A menacing bunker approximately 65 yards in front of the green comes into play for those not going for it in two. Players will approach an elevated green guarded by deep bunkers at the front and right of the green. There is a steep crest running from front right to back left. Putting from the wrong side of this crest will make for a challenging two putt par.

Number Thirteen
172 Yard Par Three

Any shot not hit within ten feet of the pin can result in a bogey. The deep bowl at the front center of this green is at least three feet lower than the back terrace. Bunkers surround almost all of this green. Perhaps a golfer's worst fate can be recovering from those bunkers behind the green and keeping the ball on the upper terrace. Proper club selection, depending where the pin is located, is a must to make birdie or par.

Number Fourteen
465 Yard Par Four

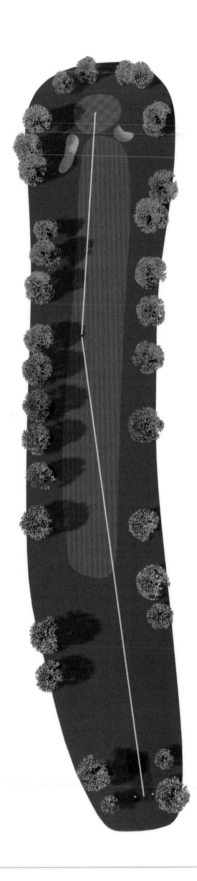

The 14th hole is the beginning of five of the toughest finishing holes in Ryder Cup history. Trees line both sides of the fairway and bunkers guard the front sides of the green, which slopes from front to back. A second shot, even if on line with the pin, can easily go through the green and into menacing rough. The 14th green has enough subtle breaks that birdies will be a rare score on this excellent hole.

Number Fifteen
399 Yard Par Four

Number fifteen is a true risk-reward hole thanks to a large bunker located in the middle of the fairway, and heavy woods just off the left edge of the fairway. If player chooses to split the fairway between the bunker and trees, he faces a shorter approach to the green. The alternative is to the right of the bunker, which will leave a much longer second shot to an elevated green that is protected by five yawning bunkers. The green is one of the more difficult putting surfaces on the course. Straight putts are rare, nor will there be an easy pin position.

Number Sixteen
409 Yard Par Four

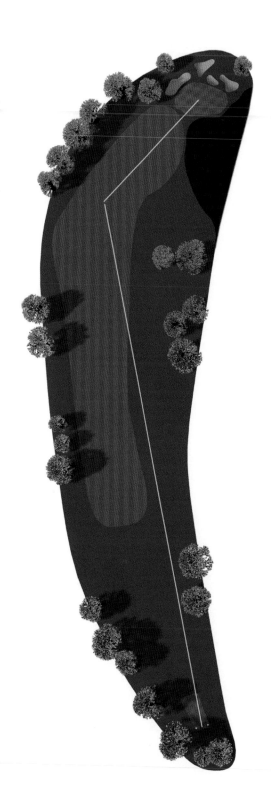

*A*nyone familiar with Oakland Hills' South Course is aware of its signature par-four hole. A wide-open fairway gives way to the most challenging second shot on the course. The wide but shallow green is guarded on the right by a large pond and is almost completely surrounded by bunkers. An approach shot which takes the pond out of play still must avoid the four surrounding bunkers. On the green, players will encounter a ridge, traveling from front to back, which makes a two-putt par a respectable score.

The 1972 PGA Championship was defined by one of the most famous clutch shots in major championship history. Coming to the 16th hole on the final day, Gary Player was tied for the lead when he pushed his tee ball behind the willows that encircle the pond guarding the green. His blind 9-iron approach cleared the willows and the water landing just four feet from the cup. He went on to birdie the hole and won the championship by two shots over Tommy Aaron.

Number Seventeen
201 Yard Par Three

his last of the par threes represents another challenge to make par. The pin will be visible in terms of left to right location but due to the green's 30-foot elevation, players cannot see how far, front to back, the pin is located. Five bunkers protect almost the entire front and sides of this green with another at the rear. Hitting the tee shot on the same side as the pin is very important given the large ridge that splits the green. Being long, or on the wrong side of the ridge, can result in bogey or worse.

On the last day of the 1985 US Open, Andy North faced a challenging shot from the deep bunker guarding the right side of the green. In the face of unrelenting pressure, North hit the shot of his life, nearly holing out from the bunker en route to his second US Open title.

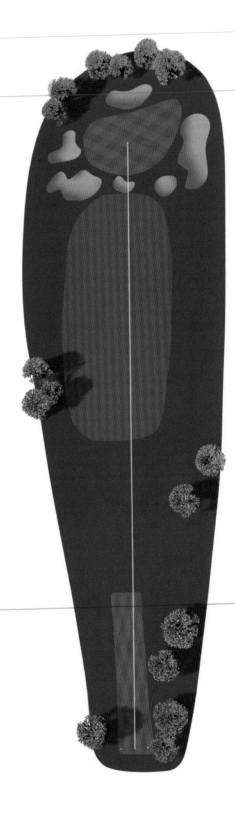

Number Eighteen
453 Yard Par Four

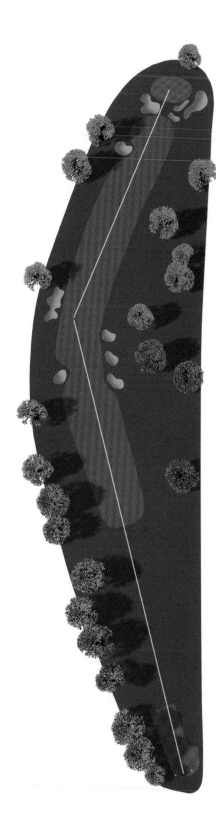

This 18th hole is one tough finishing hole. It requires an exacting tee shot and ends on the kind of green Oakland Hills is known for. The dogleg right, par-four starts from an elevated tee with out of bounds on the left, fairway bunkers at the dogleg on the right and another at the turn on the left. Players will hit their second shot to another shallow, elevated and well-bunkered green. A hump situated in the middle of the green runs from front to back and those putting from the wrong side will be challenged to avoid the dreaded three putt. Most putts from above the hole to a front pin location also make it very difficult to get down in two. For matches that go to the finish, this 18th hole will be a perfect setting for the final drama.

At the 1996 US Open, this hole was a determining factor in the demise of two contenders on the final day. Tom Lehman drilled his tee shot into the lip of the left bunker, had no shot to the green and lost his bid for the win. For Davis Love III, a two-foot down hill putt would have given him the championship. He three putted and finished runner-up the eventual winner, Steve Jones.